CREDIT CONTROL IN 90 MINUTES

C000161711

For a complete list of Management Books 2000 titles
visit our web-site on http://www.mb2000.com

CREDIT CONTROL IN 90 MINUTES

Alan Dixie FICM

2000

Copyright © Alan Dixie 2007

All rights reserved. No part of this publication may be reproduced, stored in a retrieval system, or transmitted in any form or by any means, electronic, mechanical, photocopying, recording, or otherwise without the prior permission of the publishers.

First published in 2006 by Management Books 2000 Ltd
Forge House, Limes Road
Kemble, Cirencester
Gloucestershire, GL7 6AD, UK
Tel: 0044 (0) 1285 771441
Fax: 0044 (0) 1285 771055
Email: info@mb2000.com
Web: www.mb2000.com

Printed by Chris Fowler International Ltd, London.

This book is sold subject to the condition that it shall not, by way of trade or otherwise, be lent, resold, hired out, or otherwise circulated without the publisher's prior consent in any form of binding or cover other than that in which it is published and without a similar condition including this condition being imposed upon the subsequent purchaser.

British Library Cataloguing in Publication Data is available

IBN 9781852524876

Contents

Introduction

Why do companies fail? Is it because they have got their marketing strategy completely wrong, or because their products or services are not innovative? Maybe the company has grown too quickly and is now undercapitalised? All of the above are possible, but it is far more likely that the company was simply suffering cash flow problems. How often have you read through a Liquidator's report to find that the company's order book was full, their pricing structure correct, and their costs under control. The only problem was that they couldn't collect their money quickly enough to create the cash flow needed to run the business.

If a company wants to be successful in the long term it needs to exert a firm control over the most important of its assets, the 'debtor's ledger'. Once a sale is made, customers quickly turn in to debtors, a transformation that often changes the way they are viewed by a company. However, it is vital to remember that as customers or debtors, they deserve the same level of respect and care. That's why any forward thinking company will have a well-trained credit control function to support its sales staff – working together as a team to create an interactive process that allows salespeople to sell and credit controllers to collect – which, all being equal, will result in the necessary cash flow to enable the company to prosper.

The aim of this book is to introduce you to a tried and tested system that will meet the criteria necessary to achieve the goal stated above: a credit control process that is professional in its approach, simple to administer, and most important of all, highly effective. Effective credit control is a system that will stack the odds in your favour, and could make the difference between success and failure.

1

Credit Control & Cash Flow

Why do we need credit control? Don't most people pay anyway? What difference does it make if it's today, tomorrow or next week? The answer to these often asked questions is quite simple. Collecting debt on time is important because businesses need cash flow to survive, in the same way as you or I do. If your employer decides not to pay your salary this month, how would you meet your commitments? How would you pay your mortgage or the rent on your property? How would you persuade your local supermarket to allow you to walk away with a month's shopping without paying for it? In the same way, how does a business pay its employees, its creditors, its rent and rates, without generating cash flow from the sales it makes? Okay, most of us would probably survive for a month by using a bank overdraft or savings, but what if this happened month after month? Your bank will only lend you money for so long, and even then at a high cost, which increases demands on finances you don't have. Your savings, equivalent to a company's retained earnings, will soon disappear. If your outgoings continue to exceed your income you will eventually become insolvent, just like the company that fails to collect enough cash to fund its trading costs. That's why a company needs its customers to pay when their debt is due, not next week, next month, or next year; and that is where an effective credit control team is worth it weight in gold.

At this stage I should point out that some companies are so cash rich, that they would have the resources to trade quite happily even if they were taking 90 days or more to collect their debts. However, although these companies may not be experiencing cash flow problems, they will not be maximising their profit levels either, and as a result their growth potential will suffer. This is likely to lead to a fall in the company's share price, which will not impress the shareholders who will be expecting a good return on their investment. If a company's share value falls too low it could be vulnerable to a hostile takeover.

Having looked at why an effective credit control function is necessary to create cash flow, let's take a more detailed look at the importance of cash flow, and the devastating effect that failing to control it will have on a company's trading profit.

The Importance of Cash Flow

During the recession of the 1990s, 'cash flow' became something of a buzzword. It seemed that every customer you spoke to had cash flow problems, and needed extra time to clear his account. What most of these customers were experiencing was a problem with short-term cash flow, the money a company needs on a day-to-day basis in order to trade. However, sustained cash flow is also vital if a company is to develop and grow.

The growth of any business is, to a great extent, dictated by the level of cash available to it. If, due to an ineffective credit control function, companies are forced to use their overdraft or loan capital to finance their sales function, they will find it impossible to achieve the growth necessary to survive. This inability to generate long-term cash flow usually affects smaller businesses, especially during a protracted recession, or times of high interest rates.

If businesses do not develop a long-term cash flow strategy, they will stagnate and eventually die. In the UK, the average life expectancy of a business is only ten years. If we are to increase this average, and offer the workforce greater job security, businesses need to achieve two things:

14

1. They need to control their costs.
2. They need to control their 'accounts receivable' ledger.

The higher a company's level of days sales outstanding or 'DSO' (the number of days it takes to collect its debt), the lower its cash turnover rate. This affects the level of cash flow it generates and therefore reduces the amount of retained profit, or loan capital, that is available to finance the growth of the company. Cash turnover (the rate at which debtors are converted into cash) is not only important to small businesses, which are likely to have restricted options for other types of financing; it is also an important measure for large public companies. Cash turnover offers a good measure of how well a company is being run, especially for shareholders of public companies who are not involved in the day-to-day running of the business.

The table in figure 1:1 shows the relationship between a company's DSO and its cash flow, and highlights how its cash flow can be increased through better control of its debtor base.

DSO	Cash turns (annual sales/debtors)	Improvement compared to UK average	% of annual sales released in cash compared to average
78	4.68	UK average	n/a
75	4.87	4.1%	0.8%
70	5.21	11.3%	2.2%
65	5.62	20.1%	3.6%
60	6.08	29.9%	4.9%
55	6.64	41.9%	6.3%
50	7.30	56.0%	7.7%
45	8.11	73.3%	9.0%
40	9.13	95.1%	10.4%
35	10.43	122.9%	11.8%
30	12.17	160.0%	13.2%

Fig 1:1 The relationship between a company's DSO and its cash flow

The table in figure 1:2 shows how Profits can be eroded through poor credit control. In this example Increased Profits Ltd has sales of £30,000,000; and its debtor ledger is financed by an overdraft facility at a cost of 10% per annum.

DSO	Sales	Overdraft Cost	Loss Of Additional Profit
	£	£	£
30	30,000,000	246,575	0
35	30,000,000	287,671	41,096
40	30,000,000	328,767	82,192
45	30,000,000	369,863	123,288
50	30,000,000	410,959	164,384
55	30,000,000	452,055	205,479
60	30,000,000	493,151	246,575
65	30,000,000	534,247	287,671
70	30,000,000	575,342	328,767
75	30,000,000	616,438	369,863

Fig1:2 Profit erosion through poor credit control

The Cost of Financing Credit

Everyone agrees that each day of additional credit a company extends will erode its profit, so why offer credit in the first place? The answer to this question is quite simple: a company offers its customers credit in order to maximise its level of sales. However, the initial cost of offering 30 days credit will be built into its pricing structure. Therefore, providing all its customers pay on 30 days, the company will not suffer any loss of profit. Unfortunately, in the real world people no longer pay according to terms; and every extra day of credit taken erodes the company's profit. That is why an effective credit control function is literally worth its weight in gold, and why the business graveyard is full of innovative companies who failed to control this important facet of their business. Even companies that are trading at reasonable levels of profit will eventually meet their demise if they constantly fail to control their debtor base. This problem becomes even more acute during periods of high interest rates, high inflation, or recessional pressure.

The pie chart in Figure 1:3 shows how all the various elements of extended credit can cut into the profits of a company. In this example the company is allowing 65 days credit, has a 1% bad debt provision (as a percentage of sales), and runs an average-sized credit control department. It is assumed that the company is achieving a profit after tax of 10% of sales, and is paying interest at 10%. An explanation of the calculations is set out in the following sections.

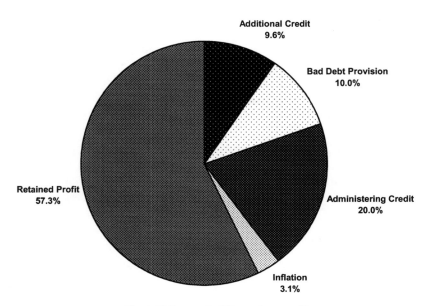

Fig 1:3 The cost of financing credit

The Cost of Financing Additional Credit

As stated above, when companies set their price levels they normally build in the associated cost of financing an initial 30-day credit period. In this example the company is taking 65 days to collect its debts, and the additional 35 days of credit are being funded through an overdraft facility. We calculate the additional cost of this credit as a percentage of profit after tax as follows. Current overdraft charge (10%), multiplied by the number of days extended credit period (35), divided by the number of days in the year (365), gives credit costs as a percentage of sales (0.96%). If we now divide this answer by the net profit margin (10%), we express the cost as a percentage of profit after tax (9.6%).

Bad Debt Provision

All businesses need to make a provision for bad debts, and the level of this provision will depend on the ability of its credit control function. Although every company will suffer some bad debts, a well run credit control function will go a long way to reducing its exposure. In the example in Fig 1:3 the company has a bad debt provision of 1 per cent of sales. The effect of the bad debt provision on profit is calculated as follows: percentage of sales (1%) divided by the profit margin (10%) equals the provision as a percentage of profit (10%).

The Cost of Administering Credit

According to surveys carried out by various trade groups, the average cost of administering credit is approximately 2 per cent of gross sales revenue. In our example this cost is calculated as a percentage of profits after tax as follows: cost of administering credit as a percentage of sales (2%), divided by the profit margin (10%), equals cost of administering credit as a percentage of profits (20%). However, it should be remembered that the longer a debt is outstanding the higher the cost of administering it. Some of these increased costs are incurred through:

- the sending out of statements
- phone calls chasing the debt
- possible collection or legal costs from third party collection companies.

Inflation

Inflation can be the silent killer, the unseen stalker waiting to pounce on the weak and poorly run company. In recent years inflation has been low and therefore not so much of a problem, but in the past, when it was running at levels of 1% per month, it had a devastating effect on companies who were failing to collect their debts within a reasonable time frame. Inflation reduces profit by reducing the purchasing power of the money collected from a company's credit sales. In Fig 1:3 the rate of inflation is calculated at 3.25 per cent per annum. Its effect on profit is calculated as follows. The inflation rate (3.25%), multiplied by the number of days extended credit (35), divided by the number of days in the year (365), gives inflation as a percentage of sales (0.31%). If you then divide this answer by the profit margin (10%), you get the inflation cost as a percentage of profit (3.1%).

High Interest Rates

During periods of high interest rates, if a company wants to maintain a high level of profit, it needs to do one of two things.

1. It can increase the price of its goods or services to cover the extended credit it is allowing to its customers. However, this will tend to lead to a reduction in sales as the company will become uncompetitive.

2. The more sensible option is for the company to collect its debt more efficiently. This process will lead to reduced borrowing levels, lowering interest payments to the bank, and resulting in an increase in retained profit.

The Effect of Credit Control on Liquidity

The simple answer to the question 'Why do we need credit control?', is so that the company can generate the liquidity it needs to survive. The liquidity of a company, is a measure of how quickly it turns its current assets into cash. As the main component of a company's current assets is its trade debtors, it follows that the liquidity of a company is dependent on its ability to collect its debts efficiently. By following the simple steps listed below the company can enhance this process.

- Sales and marketing staff must be educated on the reasons why the company needs its customers to pay promptly.
- Salespeople should make the terms of payment very clear to customers at the time a sale is made.
- There should be no delay in invoicing a sale.
- Chase action should be implemented as soon as a debt becomes overdue.
- All bad debts begin with the granting of credit. Suitable checks should be made up front on all potential customers.
- All documentation should *clearly* show the agreed price and payment terms.
- Provision for the recovery of late payment charges should be *clearly* shown on all paperwork.
- Follow a proven collection system. (See Effective Credit Control above.)
- Make sure all personnel, including sales staff, understand the company's terms and conditions of sale.

2

The Basics

What Makes a Good Credit Controller

I have spent the last 27 years managing the credit control function for three different companies, in three different industries. During this time I have worked with a large number of credit controllers, and interviewed many more – some good, some bad, and some down right ugly. But if this experience has taught me anything, it's that the interviewer needs a good understanding of the qualities he is looking for, because there are a lot of people out there who fool themselves into thinking they are good credit controllers, when in truth they are anything but. Obviously, when employing a credit controller, like any other member of staff, you will asses their character and try to judge the following:

- whether they are hard working
- whether they will work as part of a team
- whether they possess the necessary intellect to fulfil the role.

These are the basic characteristics you require of any employee, but on their own they will not guarantee you a good credit controller, so what else should you be looking for?

The Misconceptions

Age

People often hold the view that with age comes experience, and in life that is probably true, but experience doesn't necessarily bring reliability. And it certainly won't turn a bad credit controller into a good one, as age does little to change someone's underlying character, their drive, or their ability. I have worked with a number of successful credit controllers, both young and old, so age is not an issue – which is lucky, as the new EU legislation no longer allows us to discriminate by age.

Gender

I have spoken to many credit professionals over the years who have a specific take on this. There are those who believe a stern male voice will gain greater respect, and therefore make it easier for the credit controller to collect the debt. On the other hand, there are those who believe that a sweet female voice will melt the cold heart of the debtor and so produce payment. Both of these views are complete rubbish, as any self-respecting credit controller will tell you. How you approach a call should depend entirely on how your debtor is responding, it has nothing to do with your gender.

Aggression

This is one of the biggest and most costly misconceptions of all. If you learn nothing else from this book, please learn this: ***there is no place for aggression within the credit control function***. There are very few people in this world who you can frighten into paying your account, and if you try this it would probably be seen as demanding money with menace, which is a criminal offence. You persuade your debtor to pay you by remaining in control and influencing their decision. If you act in an aggressive way you are out of control, and therefore lose the power to influence. Aggressive people never make good credit controllers.

The True Qualities Required

Ability to Communicate

Communication is the key to successful credit control, the fabric onto which you stitch all the other attributes. If you are unable to communicate effectively over the phone, or through the written word, then you will never become a successful credit controller. As stated in the paragraph above, you achieve payment by influencing the debtor, and you will never achieve this if you cannot communicate effectively. Over time a credit controller can learn what to say and what not to say. They can develop an instinct as to when to apply pressure or escalate the situation. But the ability to communicate effectively is a skill; you either have it or you don't.

Persistence

On many occasions a credit controller will achieve success by wearing the debtor down. While there are ways of encouraging a debtor to pay, as discussed in later chapters, stickability pays an important role in the process. The knowledge that you will be back if payment is not received, and the fact that when you are on the phone you will not accept any excuses, will often secure you payment. This is particularly true when chasing proprietors of small businesses, who have more productive ways of spending their time.

The Ability to Remain Calm

The ability to remain calm under pressure is a vital characteristic for a successful credit controller. Debtors will often use 'attack' as their first form of defence, and it is

23

paramount that the credit controller remains calm and in control of the conversation. Sorry folks, but we are back once again to the importance of influencing the debtor. A good credit controller will possess the ability to remain focused and rise above any ploy by the debtor to drag them into an argument.

Confidence

A successful credit controller must have confidence in their ability to collect money. If they believe they are going to collect a hundred per cent of what they chase, they will probably achieve eighty per cent success. If they believe they will collect eighty per cent, they will probably achieve sixty. If they only expect to collect fifty per cent of what they chase, they should go and find themselves a new profession, because they will never succeed as a credit controller. If you don't believe in yourself the debtor will not believe in you either, and therefore you will not be able to influence his decisions.

The Role of The Credit Control Department

If I had to define the role of a credit control department in one phrase it would be 'to maximise sales and revenue while minimizing the risk of bad debt'. A simple statement but an immensely difficult task – one that requires dedication, professionalism, and a little bit of magic thrown in for good measure. I am sure there are many salespeople who would be shocked by this statement, thinking that the role of a credit controller is simply to make their life difficult. However the truth is that any successful credit control function needs to support – and in return be supported by – its sales teams. After all, we are all trying to achieve the same thing, to sell goods or services to a third party at a profit – the basic requirement for any company's survival.

In order to develop and grow, a company needs to offer credit to its customers. This is the only way it can achieve its full sales potential. Unfortunately, with the offering of credit comes the inherent risk of not being paid quickly enough to meet your cash flow requirements, or worse still, not being paid at all. Many years ago this problem hardly existed. The threat of Debtors' Prison, where the debtor would be left to rot until his family or friends could raise the necessary capital to clear his debts, acted as a good incentive to pay. But in today's manic world, with its buy-now-pay-later culture, not to mention the softening attitude of the Labour Government towards personal bankruptcy; the pendulum has swung in favour of the debtor. As a reaction to this, the last decade has seen a massive growth in the number of companies who have a dedicated credit control function.

The credit control department has two distinct roles to play: that of the 'Persuader' or the 'Enforcer'. As the 'Persuader', the credit control department will attempt to encourage the customer to pay his debt within a reasonable time frame. This form of persuasion will be carried out in a friendly and professional manner, so as not to alienate the customer and harm the prospect of further business.

Unfortunately not all customers have the intention of paying for the goods or services they receive. This type of customer will become apparent through the normal chase cycle, and at this stage the role of the credit controller changes from that of 'Persuader' to 'Enforcer'. As an enforcer the main impetus is on collecting the debt owed and not maintaining customer goodwill. At this stage it is worth stating that the enforcement process should not be undertaken until all possible avenues of payment have been explored. Enforcement action can be expensive and time-consuming, sometimes with very little reward at the end, and it will almost certainly sever any further business relationship with the customer.

Offering credit is a risky business, but it's a risk that a company needs to take if it is going to survive in today's world of commerce. A company that sells its goods or services on

25

credit is gambling that its credit controllers will collect the debt before there is no profit left in the sale. But the collecting of debt, and the need to generate further sales, present a fine balancing act – one that could determine the success or failure of the company. If a company is too lenient with its debtors it will have insufficient cash flow, and will need to borrow money, at high rates of interest, to fund the running of the business. On the other hand, if a company is too aggressive with its debt collection it will destroy its customer base, thereby reducing its level of sales. While trying to conserve this fine balance, it should be remembered that the company has taken the decision to accept the risk of selling on credit. The role of the credit control function is not to eliminate that risk but to manage it.

A Supportive System

The first requirement to allow debt to be collected efficiently is a supportive system, which can be broken down into two elements:

1. The actual hardware used in the day-to-day chase activity.
2. The support you receive from colleagues within the business.

…while the bare essentials that a credit controller requires to collect debt effectively are:

- an up-to-date debtors list,
- some form of chase history,
- a telephone.

I still come across companies that give their credit controllers no more than this. However to enhance this process it is useful also to have access to the following:

- dedicated software that allows you to draw up-to-date information from your main accounting system
- this software should also have the ability to record chase history and offer a diarised system that will bring customers back to your chase list on the required date if payment has not been made.
- the other important function for any collection system is the ability to record and maintain a history of accounts that are in query
- an integrated letter cycle
- a system that is easily configurable.

This type of system does not have to be expensive. With the help of my IT department I developed my own system at a very low cost. And if I can do it, so can you.

The Life of an Invoice

Many companies religiously measure their credit controllers' performance, setting monthly collection targets and offering bonuses to improve collection levels, but this is only part of the story. A credit controller can only have influence over a sale once it has been invoiced; therefore poor control of a company's invoicing process will quickly negate any benefits received from an effective collection system. If it takes your company thirty days to send out invoices, then the customer will effectively be receiving 60 days credit before you even start chasing the debt.

The life of an invoice begins as soon as the sales person has completed the sale, so controls should be put in place to ensure that orders are processed without delay. As the process of turning sales into cash begins with the raising of an invoice, it makes sense to set the sales ledger team targets and bonuses related to their speed and accuracy of invoicing.

An even better way to speed up the invoicing process is to harness the advantages of modern technology, and eliminate the sales ledger process altogether. If the sales departments process

27

their orders within a dedicated section of the accounting computer system, or into a sales system that has a live link to the accounting system, then the relevant invoicing data can be posted automatically to the accounts. Invoices can then be produced at the touch of a button without delay. The benefits you will achieve from this type of integrated system are threefold:

1. You will benefit from increased cash flow because the invoice is produced earlier, so that the collection process can start earlier.

2. You will reduce your staffing costs because there will be no need for a sales ledger team, who are basically duplicating the order entry process within the accounting system.

3. You will reduce the number of input errors that can lead to disputed invoices and delayed payment. There isn't a human alive who can work at one hundred per cent efficiency, therefore it follows that if fewer humans are involved within the order/invoicing process, there will be less mistakes made.

Measuring Staff Performance

As stated above, the quicker an order is processed the quicker it can be turned into cash. Therefore I believe sales ledger clerks and credit controllers should have their performance constantly monitored, and be rewarded when they achieve high levels of performance. The way I suggest monitoring these processes is as follows.

Sales Ledger Clerks

When measuring performance of the sales ledger clerks I look at three basic areas.

1. The speed that an order is turned around.

There is no point in putting processes in place to speed up the rate you receive orders from the sales departments, if it then takes three days to process these orders within sales ledger.

2. The monthly percentage of orders processed.

The target turnaround time you choose will depend on the number of orders you receive each day. I work for a magazine publishing company, and we have a continual rise and fall in the number of invoices received. There will be a large influx of invoicing at the beginning of a month, when the monthly publications are invoiced, and then again when the large weekly publications are invoiced. Because our flow of orders is not constant we set an average turnaround time that we measure at the end of each month. In addition to this we constantly review the unprocessed order situation, and keep a schedule of when orders should be received, so that we can ensure we have enough staff to meet out stated target. To encourage our staff to meet the targets set we offer a monthly bonus that is calculated as shown in the Fig 2:1on the following page.

3. The accuracy of order inputting.

There is no point in processing orders at a phenomenal rate if this is causing you to make numerous errors, because errors lead to delayed payment and increased workloads. With this in mind we keep a separate record of sales ledger errors so that we can measure the accuracy of our input clerks.

Processing Data

Business unit	Date Order Received	Number of Orders received	Date Order Processed	Orders Processed	Days	Percentage of Orders Processed	Error Rate	Error Percentage
Marketing Week	14/02/07	356	16/02/07	356	2	100%	1	0.3%
The Lawyer	15/02/07	284	16/02/07	284	1	100%	3	1.1%
Period Living	15/02/07	450	17/02/07	438	2	97%	2	0.5%
Money Marketing	16/02/07	130	17/02/07	130	1	100%	3	2.3%
Exhibitions	17/02/07	50	19/02/07	48	2	96%	1	2.1%
Events	17/02/07	35	20/02/07	35	3	100%	1	2.9%
Totals / Averages		1305		1291	2	99%	11	0.9%

Targets / Bonus Payments

Net Working Days	Bonus	Percentage of Orders Processed	Bonus	Error Percentage	Bonus	Negative Bonus
1	£85	100	£85	0.5	£85	-£20
2	£70	98	£70	1	£70	-£30
3	£50	95	£50	>1.0	£50	-£50

Fig 2:1 Processing Data Analysis

Credit Controllers

My studies have shown that the more calls a credit controller makes the greater the level of cash they collect. Even a credit controller with a poor collection technique, and I have seen a number in my time, will still collect more money by making more calls. Therefore, it follows that the first target we set our credit controllers is the number of calls they need to make each day. This target will relate to the number of calls required to complete their chase cycle within the collection month, and could be formulated as follows:

- Number of collection days in the month = 21
- Number of accounts on the Sales ledger = 1,000
- Number of accounts not falling due in month = 100
- Customers who will pay without chasing = 200
- First call success rate = 40%
- Second call success rate = 70%
- Third call success rate = 70%

Collection Process	Number of Accounts	Number of Chase Calls
Active accounts to chase	700	700
First call success rate 40%	280	
	420	420
Second call success rate 70%	294	
	126	126
Third call success rate 70%	88	
Debt Recovery Letters	38	
Total Collection Calls		1,246
Total Calls		1,246
Number of collection days		21
Number of calls per day		59

Fig 2:2 Calculation of required calls per day

31

From the table above you can see that 1,246 chase calls will need to be made during the month to complete the chase cycle, therefore this credit controller should be targeted to make 59 calls per day.

Having targeted the number of chase calls required, the next step is to target the percentage of ledger collected. There is no point in making all those calls and not collecting much debt. Once again, knowledge of your specific market, and the make-up of your customer base, will allow you to set accurate collection figures. I target collections using a collection band ranging from 55 to 65 per cent of the ledger. We pay increased levels of bonus as the percentage collected increases. This can be seen in the table in Fig 2:3 opposite.

There is one thing you have to be wary of when setting collection targets, and that is that new, large value debt, is often easier to collect. Therefore, to prevent credit controllers from concentrating solely on this debt, you should also set targets for 90-day debt levels, which must be kept below a certain percentage of the total ledger if additional bonus is to be earned.

If you calculate these target figures correctly, and supply daily updates of progress, your controllers will know exactly how they are performing and you will have a hard-working, well-motivated, and successful collection team.

Controller	Debtors Balance 31/03/07 £	Debtors Collected Apr-07 £	Percentage Collected £	Bonus Payment £	Debtors Balance 30/04/07 £	90+ Debtors Balance 30/04/07 £	90 Day Percentage £	Bonus Payment £	Total Bonus Payment £
Controller 1	1,000,000	723,000	72%	200	1,134,567	43,987	4%	50	250
Controller 2	987,567	624,876	63%	150	1,234,587	35,543	3%	100	250
Controller 3	1,243,567	745,000	60%	100	1,345,643	12,543	1%	200	300

Bonus Calculation	Total Debt Payment £	90 Day Bonus Calculation	90 Day Payment £
Total Debt		90 Day Debt	
55% Collection	50	4%	50
58% Collection	100	3%	100
61% Collection	150	2%	150
65% Collection	200	1%	200

Fig 2:3 Debt collection analysis

3

The Chase Procedure

The Psychology of Credit Control

The importance attached to the credit control function will vary from company to company, usually dependant upon the importance of their credit sales in generating the company's cash flow. For example, retail businesses such as Marks & Spencer will generate the great majority of their cash flow through cash sales and credit card transactions; credit control is not a life-threatening issue for them. In contrast, large utility companies generate most of their cash flow through credit sales, but rely on a largely automated credit control system because of the size of their customer bases; the power of their position as suppliers of essential services means they do not have to worry too much about the psychology of credit control. But for the rest of us, who need to turn our credit sales into cash quickly, *while maintaining customer goodwill*, psychology is a powerful tool that will enhance our collection potential. It is the Holy Grail of collection techniques.

The Effective Credit Control Chase Cycle

The Chase Cycle

Every credit controller will use psychology to a certain degree within his or her chase process. An example of this is the final demand letter, which acts on the debtors psyche by making him believe that something nasty is about to happen unless he clears his debt. However, this second-hand usage is not enough. To obtain the full benefits, 'chase psychology' needs to be applied in a deliberate and controlled manner. The first phase of your psychological probing will be your Chase Cycle, which should be developed in a way that will wear down your debtor's resistance, while persuading him to pay without alienating him. Studies into the effects of telephone chase cycles have shown that the optimum time lag between each element should be seven days. This allows the debtor time to think about your call, and what may happen next if payment is not made. However, the time lag between calls is not the only issue you need to consider; the content of the call is also important. If you end your chase call with the debtor feeling that you are not serious about collecting your debt, he is unlikely to worry about what will happen next, and therefore unlikely to pay. Even if the debt is only just due for payment, you still need to leave your debtor believing that you are serious about collecting your money. You should always finish your call by giving the debtor a specific date by which you expect to receive your money, as this will add the weight of expectancy to your request.

Day	Process
Invoice Date	30 Day Credit Terms
Day 31	1st Chase Call
Day 38	2nd Chase Call
Day 45	3rd Chase Call
Day 52	Debt Recovery Letter
Day 60	Third Party Action
Day 90	Instigate Legal Action

Fig 3:1 Effective credit control flow chart

36

Escalation

If the debtor fails to act by the given date, you must use that as a trigger for your next course of action. Having given the debtor a payment date, it is imperative that you progress the chase cycle if he fails to respond. He needs to know you will not go away until you receive your money. However, making the same type of chase call a second time will be of no use. You must always escalate the process if the debtor fails to respond. Having called your bluff he now needs to know that you're serious about recovering your debt, and that you're prepared to take firm action to achieve this. Once again I need to remind you that this process should be carried out in an assertive but not aggressive manner. Being assertive without being aggressive is the one quality that sorts the successful credit controllers from the also-rans.

Escalating the chase process is not only linked to the content of your call, it is also about the person you are chasing for payment. There is no point in continually making calls to the same accounts payable clerk, even if they are increasing in severity. There are two reasons for this:

1. The accounts payable clerk spends all his time fending off credit controllers and is probably quite good at it.

2. The accounts payable clerk is unlikely to be the decision maker. He does not make the decision as to when your debt gets paid.

Once you have reached this stage you need to escalate your process and start to chase the Financial Controller or Group Accountant for payment. People who operate at this level spend very little time dealing with credit controllers, and by placing these people in a position where they have to deal with this problem, you are forcing them to operate outside their comfort zone. Like everyone else they are susceptible to outside influences when not totally in control of a situation.

Harassment

Another common mistake made by the over eager credit controller is that of harassment. Continually chasing your debtor every few days may seem a good idea, but it is unlikely to bear fruit, and may even leave you open to a charge of harassment. Constant harassment will eventually lead to confrontation, where your debtor either has to lose face and give in to your demands, or take a stand as a matter of principle thereby delaying payment even longer. As it is not part of human nature to accept loss of face easily, the debtor will usually take the second option. Once the non-payment of your debt becomes a matter of principle, your debtor can convince himself he is doing all the wrong things for all the right reasons. Having allowed the situation to deteriorate in this way you are left with only one option, that of legal action. This type of enforcement is both costly and fraught with danger; and may have been avoided if a less confrontational approach had been taken.

Applying Pressure

One of the secrets of effective cash collection is to apply enough pressure on the debtor to make life uncomfortable, without pushing him over the edge. If you back any animal into a corner their natural instinct will be to attack. Giving a debtor time to consider his options may seem a waste of time, but it is actually a way of allowing him to convince himself that paying your account is his decision. It's a way of allowing the debtor to save face while still meeting your objective.

Isolation

When chasing your debtor you should try to isolate the debtor from any reasonable excuse for non-payment. By overcoming his excuses you leave him nowhere to hide, you force him to face the truth, that there is no reason to withhold payment of your debt.

Do Not Become Personally Involved

Another common error made by credit controllers is that of becoming personally involved. It's very easy to feel sympathy for the debtor who is nice and polite on the phone and openly admits he has cash flow problems, while we all dread to call the debtor who is always short-tempered, abusive, and evasive as to when we can expect payment. Both of these debtors are probably suffering from cash flow problems and therefore need to be dealt with in the same way; so why are credit controllers a lot more positive in their approach to calling Mr Nice? When chasing debt you need to look through the smokescreen, forget the personalities, and deal with the underlying problem. You should always be polite, but you need to remain detached and professional.

Listen To Your Debtor

Another important part of the psychological process is to listen to what your debtor is saying. You should never dismiss his problems as being irrelevant even if you believe they are. This type of response will put your debtor into a defensive frame of mind, which will undoubtedly result in a negative response in return. You should remain positive, sympathise with his problems and try to offer solutions that will be of benefit to you both.

Communication Skills

To be successful in life you need to be able to communicate well and credit control is no exception. You could be the brightest, most confident person in the world, but if you can't communicate you can't do this job. To be successful you need to be able to communicate over the telephone, which is one of the most powerful communication tools ever invented. To persuade your debtors to pay in accordance with your credit terms you need to influence their payment habits, and you achieve this through good communication skills. At this point it is worth remembering that you cannot influence anybody if you are out of control, so always remain calm and professional.

The Art of Communication

One of the most important facets of communication is to listen. A lot of the collection process revolves around dealing with debtor's problems, and you can't do this if you don't listen to what they are saying. Having listened, you may decide that they are just spinning you a line, and that's fine because you can now deal with them in a confident and informed manner. Rushing in before fully understanding the situation will not resolve anything. Listen, remain calm, and then act accordingly.

Communicating Over the Phone

When you communicate face-to-face with someone you have the advantage of instant feedback. Through this feedback you can judge whether you are getting your message across, and how well it is being received. When communicating via the telephone this option is not available to you, so you need to develop other skills to help you communicate clearly and effectively.

Before commencing the chase call it is worthwhile trying to find the name of the person you need to speak to. Psychologists have proved that using a person's name during your conversation works on their psyche by raising their attention level. You can use this to your advantage by raising their attention level during the important phases of your chase call. One word of warning here: do not overuse this or you will sound like a bad double-glazing salesman, and the effect will be lost.

Prepare the call in advance. A good collection call doesn't just happen, you have to put the work in up front. Make sure you read your chase history before making the call. Knowledge is power; it leads the debtor to think that you know exactly what you are talking about. Being informed leads to confidence, and confidence leads to good communication.

Communication By Email

Email, as its name suggests, is an electronic form of a letter, it is not a replacement for the telephone. Too often I see credit controllers trying to have a conversation by email. If you want a conversation with your debtor, *pick up the phone*, do not use email. Conversations through email tend to be abrupt and easily misinterpreted. It's not what you say but the way that you say it that counts. Email is a great tool for confirming what was said in a conversation, or enabling you to reply instantly to a debtor in a written format. It is great for sending invoices or statements to a debtor, with no risk of them getting lost in the post. It can be a powerful communication tool too but you need to recognise its limitations. Finally, never, never, never use text speak in an email. It is unprofessional, and if the recipient is anything like me they won't waste their time trying to work out what you are saying.

Communication By Letter

The letter has the advantage of providing a hard copy of the communication between yourself and your debtor. This is useful if you need to proceed with legal action for the recovery of your debt. It is also a useful tool for raising the stakes in the chase process, i.e. the Final Letter, or as I prefer, the Debt Recovery Letter. Although email is starting to supersede the written letter, there is something about a letter physically arriving on your debtor's desk that works on his psyche. Any chase letter you send should be concise. Don't waffle or use flowery sentences. And please, never finish a chase letter with the phrase, *'if you have recently sent payment please ignore this letter'*. This suggests you are either inefficient at allocating the payments you receive, or uncomfortable about chasing the debt, both of which a professional debtor will use against you. If payment has not been received at the time you send the letter,

41

then you have every right to follow that course of action, don't apologise for doing so. On occasions payments do cross in the post; there is nothing you can do about that.

The Chase Calls

When chasing for payment, making a well-prepared chase call is not enough, you also need to make it to the right person. This may sound stupid, but believe me it is one of the most common mistakes made when chasing overdue debt. There is no point in spending five minutes convincing an accounts payable clerk that your account should be paid if they do not have the authority to pay it. You need to make sure you are talking to a 'decision maker', the person who has the authority to make payment. In a large company, providing your invoice has been approved by the business, this may well be the accounts payable clerk. If this is the case then you should work at developing a good working relationship with this person. However, if you are dealing with a small family run business, it is unlikely that the accounts lady, who only works Tuesdays and Thursdays, has the authority to make payment. In this scenario it is much more likely to be the proprietor who makes the decision, so that's the person you need to speak to.

Call One

In your first collection call you should adopt a polite and pleasant attitude. Your debt may be overdue for payment, but that doesn't mean your debtor is trying to avoid payment. Some people simply need a gentle reminder to encourage them to pay. In this call, provided it is made as soon as the debt is due, your customer will expect to be given the benefit of the doubt. The last thing you want to do is alienate your good customers by reacting in the wrong way to their request for a copy invoice or proof of delivery.

As a rule of thumb, you should not need to '*get tough*' in your first chase call, unless the debtor says something that

42

makes it quite clear he has no intention of paying your account. A tough approach in your first call may increase your collection success rate, but credit control is not that easy; it is not simply about collecting debt at any cost. At this stage your debtor is still a valued customer, and there is no sin in trading a few days extra credit against the prospect of future sales.

Call Two

The second call you make will be the most important call of the three. The first thing to remember is to progress the chase process. There is no point in simply repeating your first call, because you won't achieve success without progression. Once again, please remember that you do not progress the chase cycle by being rude or aggressive, there is no place for these stances in effective credit control. In call two you need to be more assertive, and you achieve this by using the powerful techniques of reversing arguments, and overcoming false logic, both of which are discussed fully in the next chapter.

Even though you may have progressed the call in the right way, there are still no guarantees that the debtor will send a cheque, however, the chances of receiving payment will have been greatly enhanced. Your debtor is now aware that you are not going to give up, and that is an important step in the psychological process. Having got that message across, and providing your debtor has the money to pay you, you will probably receive a cheque within seven days.

Call Three

By this stage of your chase cycle most of your customers will have cleared their accounts, and for those that haven't, any requests for copy invoices, excuses, or grievances should have been resolved. This means the debtors who still owe you money will now fall into one of two categories: those who cannot pay you, and those who will not pay you until they are forced to. Your first task is to decide which category your debtors fall in to, as you will need to react differently to each of these problems.

The third call is what I like to call the crystal ball call. In this call you explain to your debtor the situation as it stands at present, then predict his future if your account remains unpaid. Most important of all, you must make it clear to the debtor that this problem is of his making, and that it is his decision as to how things progress from here.

The third call is unique as it consists of one hundred per cent power. Because of its content it is also the most volatile of the three calls, and as such needs to be handled carefully. Control and professionalism is still of the utmost importance. This is definitely not a situation where you can blast away indiscriminately without thought or cohesion. Despite the content of the call you still need to influence the debtor if you are to be successful, and as we all know you cannot influence someone if you are out of control.

If your debtor has no money to pay you, all the threats in the world are not going to change that. At this stage you need to seriously discuss payment proposals with your debtor. However, if your debtor does have the money, but is simply refusing to pay, then you need to explain the consequences of his actions, which will include the following.

- payment of legal costs and statutory interest on top of the original debt
- loss of credit rating for seven years
- the cost of time wasted fighting legal action
- the possibility of being forced into liquidation or bankruptcy.

Throughout your collection process you should make it clear to your debtors that the actions you are taking are as a result of their actions. You should always try to be conciliatory wherever possible, but never leave the debtor in any doubt that you are prepared to take tough action if necessary to recover your debt.

Collection Letters

I am a strong believer in collection letters when used in conjunction with telephone calls, but I do not believe that a chase cycle derived entirely of a series of letters is an effective way of collecting debt. It may work for the large utility companies who have hundreds of thousands of customers and therefore need a cost effective way of collecting their debt. As a general rule the collection process for these companies is not designed for customer retention, and therefore does not need to offer a personalised customer service. For the rest of us, who have to work hard at customer retention, I would suggest using chase letters sparingly. My collection team only use one letter, which is sent out at the end of the collection cycle, prior to handing the account out to a collection agency. However, there is nothing wrong in sending a letter out between your second and third chase calls, but note that this will extend the length of your chase cycle by seven days. Examples of these letters are listed below.

Interim Chase Letter

Dear Mr Smith.

Despite our previous request for payment of your account, we note that there is still an overdue balance as detailed below.

Our terms and conditions clearly state that all invoices must be paid within thirty days of invoice date. WE MUST NOW INSIST ON PAYMENT OF ALL OVERDUE INVOICES WITHIN SEVEN DAYS.

Failure to act on this matter could lead to the suspension of your credit facilities, a statutory late payment interest charge, and ultimately lead to legal action being taken to recover the debt.

We await your payment by return

The Debt Recovery Letter

Dear Mr Smith.

Overdue Balance £1,234.65

Despite repeated requests for payment of your account we regret to note that the overdue balance still remains unpaid.

We had hoped that this matter could have been resolved amicably between ourselves, but as your attitude appears to render this impossible, we now intend to instigate third party collection action by passing your account out of hand to our Debt Recovery Agency.

Should this course of action fail to bring about the desired results then legal action will be commenced against you without further reference to yourselves.

In accordance with our standard terms and conditions of sale, upon handing your account out to a third party for collection the entire balance of your account, including any current invoicing, will be deemed due and payable immediately. Late payment interest will also be levied on top of the balance listed above.

Our final letter is sent out on good quality grey paper and headed up Debt Recovery Enforcement Department. This creates a strong visual impact and works on the debtor's psyche, leading him to realise that things have escalated. When we make our last collection call we state that if payment is not made the account will be passed out to our debt recovery section, so the letter heading is designed to tie the two elements together and helps to achieve that all important escalation process.

Credibility

One of the most important rules in credit management is always to appear credible to your debtor. The debtor must believe that if you threaten a certain course of action you will carry it through. This is why working together with the sales team is so important. A united front is essential if you are to achieve credibility.

To recap, the four elements necessary for successful debt collection are:

1. A progressive chase cycle.
2. An effective and supportive system.
3. Confidence.
4. Credibility.

$$4$$

Overcoming Excuses

Excuses are a debtor's stock-in-trade, their escape route to delay or prevent payment of your account. As a successful credit controller you will need to know how to deal with these excuses in an effective and professional way. Tearing through a debtors excuse without any thought is akin to charging through a minefield without a mine detector. Debtors are clever and devious and you need to arm yourself with the tools to counter this. And because it's your responsibility to generate your company's cash flow, this is one battle you can't afford to lose.

Before we look at how to overcome excuses, perhaps we should examine exactly what an excuse is. An excuse is often just an emotional reaction to an event or problem that threatens us or our standing. If something goes wrong what is the first thing we do? Instinctively we try to find an excuse to explain away our error, to save face. A debtor is no different; if you try to force him to pay he will search for an excuse to explain why he can't. In the world of commerce this emotional reaction usually manifests itself from three sources:

1. A debtor's fear of not being able to clear his debts
2. A debtor's greed
3. A debtor's dislike for the company or person he is dealing with.

The difficulty for the credit controller is in spotting this emotional response. As I said, debtors are devious, and they entangle the emotional response in false logic, which, on the surface, can seem quite logical. To overcome excuses you need to follow a simple process:

- soothe the emotion behind the excuse
- state the true logic
- and only as a last resort, apply power.

The three elements of this process are now discussed in greater detail.

Overcoming the False Logic

When a debtor offers an excuse for not paying your account, your job is to turn the tables on him and make the payment of your account his easiest option. While the false logic of the debtor's excuse may be clear to see, the emotion attached to the excuse is real, and therefore needs to be dealt with before you can progress. At this stage the uninitiated credit controller will make the mistake of acting in one of two ways:

1. He will start to argue with the debtor's false logic.
2. He will make a power play in order to resolve things quickly.

Both of these responses are wrong and will only lead to further delays in payment. For example, arguing with your debtor's false logic will allow him to sidetrack you, taking you further and further away from your desired goal, the payment of your account. This type of argument could progress something like this:

(Debtor) "I can't tell you if I have sent you a cheque or not as my books are with my accountant."

(Collector) "Surely your accountant realises you need access to your records. Why is he not auditing your accounts in your office?"

50

(Debtor) "My accountant works from home. I think you're being unreasonable as this doesn't cause a problem with any of my other suppliers."

(Collector) "I can't believe this has never caused you a problem before. I am sure your other suppliers need to be paid on time as well."

(Debtor) "Well I'm telling you that you are the only supplier who has a problem with this. I run a small business here; this is not unusual practice for a business of my size."

In situations like this, the more you argue with the debtor the further away you get from securing payment. However, if you choose to apply power without first soothing the emotion and stating the true logic, you will also have problems. Applying this approach, the call may go something like this:

(Debtor) "I can't tell you whether I have paid your invoice or not because my books are with my accountant at present."

(Collector) "Mr Smith we both know I can't accept that. You must know whether you have paid our account or not."

(Debtor) "I deal with a lot of suppliers, I can't remember all the cheques I have issued. Can you remember all the cheques you have received without referring to your records?"

By applying power too soon you are only going to aggravate your debtor. Nobody likes to be called a liar, and at this stage you don't really know if you debtor is telling the truth or not. In situations like this you have to unravel the truth from the emotion, by stating the true logic and monitoring you debtor's reaction. It's not always easy to distinguish truth from emotion; that's why debtors use this type of delaying tactic.

Soothing the Emotion

When a debtor comes at you with false logic your first action has to be to soothe the emotion attached to that false logic. This means that you do not ignore the emotion or argue with your debtor; you simply sympathise with his predicament and then state the true logic of the situation. By sympathising with the debtor you are not agreeing to his excuse; you are simply acknowledging it and then bypassing his excuse by stating the true logic. This process takes a little time to master, but once you are comfortable with it you will find that your chase calls do not deteriorate into arguments, and therefore your success rate will increase.

Stating the True Logic

In order to ascertain whether your debtor does have a genuine problem you have to examine his reasoning, and you do this by asking questions designed to open up the discussion. If carried out correctly, your call to Mr Smith should go something like this:

> (Debtor) "I can't tell you whether I've paid my account or not because my books are with my accountant." (*False Logic*)

> (Collector) "I appreciate your problem Mr Smith. (*Soothing the Emotion*) How long will your accountant be working on them?" (*True Logic*)

> (Debtor) "I think he will be working on them for the next two weeks." (*False Logic*)

> (Collector) "I'm sure you appreciate Mr Smith that two weeks is a long time for you to be without your records." (*Soothing the Emotion*) "Is there any chance you could phone your accountant and check whether our account for £3,000 still remains unpaid?" (*True Logic*)

(Debtor) "That may be possible, if you leave it with me I will see what I can find out and call you back." (*Capitulation*)

(Collector) "Thank you for your co-operation Mr Smith. It is most appreciated. I will diarise your account for review on Friday, by which time you should have come back to me." (*Letting the debtor know what you expect of him and that if he doesn't take action you will be back on his case.*)

By approaching the call in this way you have avoided any unproductive arguments, and extracted a promise from Mr Smith to sort something out. You have also planted the idea in his mind that if he doesn't sort something out you will be back on the phone wanting to know why.

The Power Phase

The power phase is the most dangerous and destructive of the three elements, and as such should only be used when all other options have failed. Once you have made a power move there is no way back to the previous two options. When making a power move you should always make the debtor aware that you don't want to take this action, and it's his decision as to what happens next.

If we follow through with our previous call and assume Friday arrives without any contact from Mr Smith, the power call should go something like this:

"(Debtor) "I have not had a chance to speak to my accountant yet. I should be speaking to him within the next few days."

(Controller) "Mr Smith, when we spoke earlier in the week you promised me that you would resolve this problem by today. This debt is already approaching sixty days of age, Mr Smith. We can't afford to wait any longer for payment."

(Debtor) "I'm sorry, but as I have already stated I need to speak to my accountant before I can pay your account."

(Controller) "Then I must ask you to speak to him and resolve this within the next forty eight hours Mr Smith. If you don't, you leave us with no option other than to proceed with legal action for the recovery of your debt. It seems so silly that our trading relationship should come to this. Is this really what you want to happen, Mr Smith?"

At this stage this call could go one of three ways. First Mr smith could admit that he has a cash flow problem, in which case you can negotiate some form of payment plan to clear your debt. Secondly, Mr Smith could remain elusive during the rest of the conversation, but having had time to weigh up the alternatives decides to send a cheque. Lastly Mr Smith could remain belligerent, deciding he will not pay the account until he deems fit, in which case you will have to proceed with enforcement action to recover your debt.

Overcoming Common Excuses

This is a credit controller's stock-in-trade, the area where they spend most of their time. The ability to turn sales into hard cash is a prerequisite to success, and overcoming excuses is the one process that really sorts the good from the bad. I have listed below some of the more common excuses and how to overcome them.

No-One Is Available to Sign the Cheque

At the outset it is difficult to know whether this is a case of true or false logic. In order to clarify the situation you need to probe this response in the following way:

(Controller) "When will Mr Smith be returning to the office?"

If Mr Smith will be returning tomorrow then this is probably true logic, in which case you can ask the accounts payable clerk to organise a payment for Mr Smith to authorise on his return. You can then re-enforce this request by stating that you will call

54

Mr Smith tomorrow morning to ensure there are no problems with authorising payment.

However, if the reply to your question is that Mr Smith will be out of the office for four weeks, then it is safe to assume this is false logic, in which case you need to soothe the emotion and state the true logic in the following way.

> (Controller) "I appreciate your problem if Mr Smith is going to be away for so long, but I presume he must have made some provision for paying overdue accounts in his absence."

If the clerk continues to insist that no provision has been made to pay overdue debts, you should once again soothe the emotion and state the true logic in the following way:

> (Controller) "I appreciate how difficult that must be for you, but can you tell me who is authorising your salary and utility payments?"

If Mr Smith is really going to be away for four weeks it is very unlikely that he hasn't made provision to cover the payment of certain debts, therefore you need to continue to probe until the clerk admits that Mr Smith has left some cheques to clear urgent bills. (This means he is only to send them out as a last resort if he has been unable to stall the supplier. And of course, because you're persistent, and willing to make a power play if necessary, you will get paid.)

The Computer System Is Down

As technology advances, so does this debtor's excuse, which is fast becoming the modern day equivalent of 'the cheque is in the post'. Unfortunately computer systems do malfunction, so this could be a genuine excuse. To clarify things you need to probe further:

> (Controller) I'm sorry to hear that. I know what a problem that can be. Is this a common problem with your system?"

(Clerk) "It's not a constant problem but it does happen every now and again."

(Controller) "I assume someone from I.T. is trying to resolve the problem, but can you tell me how long the system is usually down for?"

(Clerk) "From past experience it usually takes about a week to rectify the problem."

Now that you have a firm timeframe to work with you can make your next move. If the company is genuinely having problems, and they are going to be without a system for a week, they will be willing to send you a manual payment. This is especially true of larger organisations that will almost certainly have a payment run every week, and some form of back-up procedure. If the debtor refuses to make payment then they are obviously trying to delay payment and you will need to make a power play to recover your money.

The Cheque Is In the Post

This excuse is right up there with 'Of course I will still love you in the morning darling', and 'Hello, I'm from head office, I've come to help you'. It is one of the great lies of our time. Unfortunately, once again, this excuse could be either true or false, but if you approach things correctly it will only buy your debtor a further 48 hours credit. Within this time frame you will know, one way or the other, whether your debtor was telling the truth.

During this call you should work into the conversation the following questions, all of which the debtor should be able to answer if he has sent the cheque:

- What is the cheque number?
- What was the value of the cheque?
- What address was it sent to, and for whose attention?
- Was the cheque sent first or second class?

If you end your call armed with this information then you can be fairly confident that the cheque is in the post. However, as always, you should end the call by making the debtor aware, as nicely as possible, that if payment is not received within a couple of days, you will be back on the phone.

If the cheque does not arrive, then the cheque has either been lost, in which case a replacement needs to be issued, or the debtor has lied to you, in which case you need to make a power play. If the debtor is sending you a replacement cheque you should ask for the new cheque number, and compare it to the previous cheque number the debtor gave you to make sure they are in the same sequence. If the debtor lied about the original cheque number they probably won't be, and therefore you need to question him about this. Putting the debtor on the spot won't change the fact that he lied to you, but it will let him know that you are on-the-ball, and serious about collecting your money.

The Elusive Mr Smith

If Mr Smith is unavailable every time you try to contact him, and refuses to return your call, then he is obviously trying to delay, or even worse, evade making payment. However, don't despair. All may not be lost. If Mr Smith works for a large organisation there may be a way to catch him. You should proceed to phone the company in the normal way, but when you get through to the switchboard you should ask for someone else within the organisation (someone on the sales side tends to work fairly well). When they answer the phone ask to speak to Mr Smith. Nine times out of ten the person at the other end of the line will say, 'I'm sorry you have been put through to the wrong extension, I will transfer you'. They usually transfer you direct to Mr Smith's extension and not to the person who is screening his calls. If you are really lucky they will give you his direct extension number.

Having got through to Mr Smith you need to make the most of the opportunity, so you should proceed straight away with a power call. This may be the only chance you have of speaking to Mr Smith, so you need to leave him in no doubt as to the seriousness of the situation. Providing you left messages for Mr Smith during your previous calls, he will be aware of the debt you are chasing, and have no excuse for not getting back to you.

Reversing Arguments

Not all debtors hide their true intentions behind false logic when trying to delay payment; some believe the best form of defence is attack. This type of debtor usually has an arrogant approach, and tries to make you feel uncomfortable or unimportant when you call him. He does this in the hope that you will think twice before you call again, but we know better, don't we! In situations like this you need to be assertive to take control of the situation, but be careful – there is nothing this type of debtor likes more than an argument – something he can run and complain about to the sales manager.

The way to deal with this debtor is to turn his excuses on himself, and use the basis of his excuse to make it difficult to avoid payment. 'Reversing arguments' are effective because they are assertive without being rude or offensive. They use the debtor's own argument to secure payment, and leave the debtor with the option of paying or arguing against his own logic. As this type of debtor does not like losing face he would rather pay than be made to look a fool, and once you get a debtor thinking in this way you are a long way towards succeeding. I have listed below some examples of how reversing arguments can be used to overcome excuses.

I'm Too Busy

If your debtor replies to your chase call by saying,

> (Debtor) "I'm sorry, but I'm too busy to deal with this problem now"

...your reversing argument should be:

(Collector) "I appreciate how busy you are Mr Smith, and I promise I will be brief".

By arguing with this, Mr Smith would be saying that he didn't want you to be brief, he would also be wasting his precious time, which defeats his original excuse. The quickest way out of this problem would be for Mr Smith to promise payment of your account.

I Need a Copy Invoice

Despite what people want to believe, our postal system is one of the best in the world, and only a very small fraction of mail actually goes missing, but it's funny how it always seems to be *your* invoices and cheques which get 'lost'. Do the invoices jump up and down in the sorting office screaming, 'I'm an invoice, I'm an invoice, lose me'. I think not, which can only mean one thing: God forbid, our debtors are lying to us.

As you build up a debtor's chase history it will become apparent if a debtor is using lost invoices as an excuse to delay payment. If this is the case you should deny them any further extension in the following way:

(Debtor) "I am waiting for a copy invoice before I can pay your account. I have requested copies before."

(Controller) Is this the only thing preventing you from paying your account Mr Smith?"

(Debtor) "Yes."

(Controller) "I will fax or email a copy over to you straight away. I presume from what you have just stated Mr Smith, that you will now be able to send a cheque today for the full value."

By turning the tables on Mr Smith, and getting him to agree that the only thing preventing him from paying your account was the need for a copy invoice, he has backed himself into a corner. He either has to pay your account, or admit that his requests for copy invoices are nothing more than a delaying tactic. As stated earlier, humans do not like to lose face, so the easiest option for Mr Smith is to pay your account.

A way to eliminate this excuse all together is to send all your invoicing by email, rather than post. There are a number of benefits in doing this:

- Invoices never get lost.
- The debtor receives invoices instantly.
- Your company saves on paper and postage costs.

The Cheque Must Have Got Lost in the Post

As stated earlier, very little gets lost in the post, so on hearing this excuse the chances are that either you have in fact received the payment but not allocated it correctly, or the debtor is lying.

In most cases when a credit controller is faced with this scenario they ask the following questions:

- When did you send the cheque?
- Where did you send the cheque?
- What was the value of the cheque?
- What is the cheque number?

All of these questions are valid if you need to trace what has happened to the cheque your end, but do not require your debtor to do anything further. You now have to try and trace the payment your end, which if you work for a large organisation could take some time, only to find you haven't received it. It makes much more sense to make your debtor do the work, especially as they know whether they are lying or not. So the first question you need to ask is:

(Controller)   "Has the cheque cleared your bank yet?"

Your debtor can find this out within thirty minutes, and what is more they have to tell the truth, because when they call you and say the cheque has cleared you are going to ask them:

- What date did the cheque clear your bank?
- Which bank was it presented through?
- What date was it presented?
- Could you supply a copy of the front & back of the cheque?

Another way to prevent this excuse ever arising is to ask your debtor to pay you by BACS. It will be less time consuming for them, and you know payments will never get lost.

Reversing arguments usually tie the debtor down to the option that makes him take action straight away. They succeed because they are assertive, and they are assertive because you place the onus back on the debtor. He has to make a decision, and providing you have played your hand correctly, the simplest option for your debtor should always be to pay your account.

5

Maintaining Influence Over Your Debtor

Every day credit controllers across the country are facing the same problem: how to collect debt as quickly as possible, but without damaging the trading relationship that exists with the customer. Customer goodwill is an important factor for any successful company and must be nurtured wherever possible. The most effective, and least confrontational way to collect debt is to influence your debtor's payment habit. As a credit controller there are basically two ways to achieve this:

1. Through the language you use during the call
2. Through the actual content of the call.

You should always take grate care with the language you use when making your chase call. If you use language that puts your debtor on the defensive, or worse still causes him to turn off altogether, you are seriously affecting the impact of your influencing strategy. The content of your call can be well thought out and influential, but if your debtor has mentally switched off it will have no effect.

People can be alienated as easily as they can be influenced. The right thing said in the wrong way can lead to confrontation, lost objectives, and more importantly, the loss of a valued customer. In the past, debtors felt a personal need to honour their debt but sadly this is no longer the case. In today's world of commerce you will need to find a way of manipulating your debtors' commercial need to pay you, rather than just remind them that the debt is overdue.

Despite what you may be told in numerous training videos, there is no such thing as a uniform debtor. Your customers are all unique and the way you influence them will vary, the secret being to match the correct influencing factor to the correct debtor. Some of your debtors will only need the gentlest of encouragement to pay, while others will need a firm line taken from the start. It's important, where possible, to get to know your debtors, and to learn how to satisfy their needs while meeting your objectives. You need to keep this concept at the front of your thought process when making a collection call. Your debtor is only interested in his needs and not yours, so phrases like 'we need your cheque today' or 'we need to pay our suppliers too' are of no interest to him and will not secure payment.

Making the Call

Before you can influence a debtor's payment pattern, you have to know what his needs are, and the only way to obtain this information is to converse with him. By asking questions and listening to his response you will be able to assess his needs, and therefore select the correct influencing factor to satisfy them. When making a collection call you also need to remain positive at all times, not only in your thought process, but also through the language you use. If you convince your debtor that you want to find a solution that will satisfy everyone, he in return is far more likely to respond positively to your suggestions.

Matching a debtor to his correct influencing factor requires a little practice, but to help in this quest I have listed below some of the more common influencing factors, and when and how they should be used.

Suspension of Credit

If you asked a hundred credit controllers to state the first influencing factor that came to mind, ninety-five of them would think of this one. In fact, I would go as far as saying that in half the credit control departments in the country, this is the only influencing factor used. It is general practice within the industry to send out standard chase letters, which usually refer to the suspension of credit facilities. Because these letters are an embedded part of the chase process they will be sent to all overdue debtors, irrespective of whether they are still trading with the company. This type of blanket usage will be unproductive against those customers who are currently not trading with you. As a result the suspension of credit letter has lost some of its impact as an influencing factor.

The suspension of a customer's credit facilities will only have an affect on those customers who buy your goods or services on a regular basis, and then only if the supply of these goods or services affects the profitability of their own company. The greater your customer's need for your goods or services, the stronger the impact of this influencing factor.

It is possible that some of your debtors will have more than one need to fulfil. If this is the case you should always work on the greatest need. The greater your customer's need, the greater the power of your influencing factor, and the greater the level of your success.

Credit Rating

Credit rating can be used as either a positive or a negative influencing factor, and the way in which you choose to use it will depend on the relationship you have with your customer. For example, if your customer uses your company on a regular basis for trade references, he will have a strong need for you to report positively on his company. This is a powerful need that can be exploited to speed up the payment of your account. In this example you are satisfying Mr Smith's need for good trade references, while fulfilling your objective of being paid on time.

The use of 'credit rating' as a negative influencing factor, occurs where you are trading with a customer who does not consider payment of your account to be a priority. An example of this might be where a customer runs a weekly advertising campaign lasting one month. Having had the benefit of the advertising, and having no particular need to advertise again in the near future, he does not feel any need to give priority to the payment of our account. In this type of scenario I would suggest you try to influence the debtor in the following way.

> (Collector) "I appreciate that the payment of our account may not be a priority for you, Mr Smith, however I feel I should inform you that we do supply payment information to the leading business information companies on a monthly basis. Any delay in the payment of our account, Mr Smith, will be reported and could affect the credit rating they give your company."

Although Mr Smith may feel he has no immediate need to pay your account, he will undoubtedly have suppliers who are important to him, both now and in the future. By using this influencing factor in a negative way you are feeding on Mr Smith's need to maintain a good credit rating to satisfy your objective of receiving payment. If Mr Smith already has a poor credit rating this influencing factor will not work, and you will need to use the threat of legal action to recover your debt.

To Get You Off Their Backs

This influencing factor works wonderfully on those customers who are too busy to spend time arguing with you over the payment of your account. This usually means small businesses rather than medium or large sized businesses, which will employ dedicated accounts payable clerks to deal with annoying people like us.

When chasing payment from smaller businesses, you will almost certainly be talking to the proprietor, and as such his time could be spent more productively than discussing the payment of your debt. This type of debtor is often aggressive in his response when you initially call, hoping to frighten you into not calling again. However, once it becomes clear that you will not go away, the easiest option for him is to pay your account and get you off his back. One word of warning here, make sure you do not cross that thin line between persistence and harassment.

Credit Limits

This influencing factor can only work on a customer who depends on the supply of your goods or services for the continuation of his business. In this circumstance the level of credit offered to the customer is like a lifeline, and as such makes a very powerful influencing factor.

This customer will also be a regular customer and as such also vulnerable to the 'suspension of credit' influencing factor. However, trying to influence your customer's payment habit through credit limits has two important advantages:

1. By using the 'credit limit' influencing factor, you will maintain a more harmonious trading relationship with your customer. Just because your customer has reached his credit limit it doesn't necessarily mean he has done anything wrong. Therefore, he should not become defensive when advised of the situation.

2. As you are not accusing the debtor of any wrongdoing, you can use this influencing factor at any stage of your chase cycle, even before normal credit terms have expired. If this approach is unsuccessful you still have the option of suspension of credit.

Increased Costs

This influencing factor will work on any of your debtors to a certain degree, but will be most effective on those who are cash managing your money. You can tell when a debtor is cash managing your money because they will use closed excuses when trying to delay payment. Closed excuses are where the excuse has a finite time. An example of this would be where a debtor states, "We always pay our accounts on 60 days." This type of debtor does have the money to pay your account, but they would rather keep it in their own bank account, and use your money to finance the running of their business.

This influencing factor has a positive and negative approach. On the positive side you can offer your customers a prompt payment discount. This may prove attractive to debtors who have the funds to clear your account, but are withholding payment to improve their own trading position.

Unfortunately it will not work in its positive form on debtors who do not have the funds to clear your account. You can spot this type of debtor because they use open-ended excuses when delaying payment. This is an excuse that has no definite end date. An example of such an excuse is, 'the cheque is in the post', or 'I need a copy invoice'.

On the negative side, this influencing factor can be used as a penal charge for late payment, which should be included in your terms and conditions of sale, although your statutory right to make a late payment charge has now superseded this process. Companies often instigate this charge to coincide with sending the debtor's account out to a third party for enforcement action.

You must remember that this influencing factor has to be used on a decision-maker; it will not work on an accounts payable clerk. They have very little influence over when your account is paid, and even less interest in additional costs their company may have to pay.

Legal Action

There is no doubt that the threat of legal action can focus a debtor's mind, especially if they know they don't have a valid reason for withholding payment of your account. In this respect it can certainly be considered an influencing factor. However, I see legal action as the end game when all other forms of influence have failed. If you have reached this stage without receiving payment, it usually means that your debtor has no funds available to clear your debt, or that he intends to make you work very hard to get your hands on his money. If he is experienced in the workings of the legal system, he can tie your money up for many months before having to pay up. Very rarely is this a quick process for recovering your money, so make sure you are prepared for the long haul before proceeding with this action.

If you are using a three-call chase cycle, all of the other influencing factors should have been used in your first two chase calls. The threat of legal action can be costly and therefore should only be used as a final gambit, which means it will only be used in your last chase call. Once you have threatened legal action there is no way back.

As previously stated, there is no collection system in existence that is a perfect panacea; and the use of influencing factors is no exception. However, provided your debtor does intend to pay your account at some stage, and hopefully most of them do, then the use of influencing factors will speed up the point at which your debtor pays. I have included an 'influencing factors' quick reference table at the end of this chapter, so that you can match the correct influencing factor to the correct type of debtor.

The use of influencing factors, harnessed with the process of overcoming excuses, will create a powerful collection process that will reduce the length of time it takes to collect your debts. This process is assertive without being aggressive, and therefore will allow you to achieve your goal of maximising sales while minimising bad debts. It should also result in a greater level of customer retention.

The role of the credit controller has definitely evolved over the last decade. The modern day controller needs to be multifaceted, and able to think quickly. No matter what type of debtor you are dealing with, somewhere within the last three chapters is the key to unlocking their payment potential. The difficulty comes in matching the correct process to the correct debtor, while remaining flexible in your approach. The only exception to this will be the debtor who is basically a crook, and fortunately these debtors are few and far between.

Influencing Factors
Quick Reference Guide

Influencing Factor	Type of debtor it works on
Suspension of credit	Any debtor who buys your goods or services on a regular or continuous basis.
Credit rating positive	Debtor who uses your company on a regular basis for credit references.
Credit rating negative	Debtor who does not see your goods or services as important to him, but does need to maintain a good credit profile. If your debtor does not care about his credit rating this influencing factor will not be effective.
Get you off their backs	Small businesses where the proprietor's time would be better spent on other priorities.
Credit Limit	Debtor who depends on your goods or services for the continued existence and growth of his business.
Increased costs	Useful against all debtors, through cash discounts for prompt payment, or surcharges for slow payment. (Most effective against debtors who are cash managing your money.)
Legal action	The final action to be used against your debtors when all other options have been exhausted.

6

Collection Agencies & Solicitors

No matter how vigorous your credit vetting procedures are, or how experienced your credit control team is, there will always be debt that is uncollectable in-house – the 'can't pay' and 'won't pay until you make life difficult for me' brigade. I have worked with credit controllers who have wasted copious amounts of time making unsuccessful chase calls to these types of debtor, while the more initiated accept the situation and make the final escalation gambit. How can anyone justify making numerous chase calls, all of which should be progressive, to the same customer? What on earth could you say in each call that would make them unique? If you're good at your job, three calls, four at a maximum, is all you need. By this stage you will know whether you are going to collect the debt or not. If not, hand it out to a third party. It's the only way to escalate things further and maintain the pressure on your debtor.

Having progressed through your chase cycle without success, you have reached the point where the ultimate escalation is required. You need to hand your debt out to a third party for collection, but whom do you use? Some people proceed immediately to legal action, believing that a collection agency will have no more success in collecting the debt than their own credit controllers. Based on my experience I would say this is definitely not the case. A letter or phone call from a collection agency has a proven psychological affect on your debtor. The intervention of a third party suggests that matters have escalated, and most of those 'won't pay until you make life difficult for me' debtors are realising the game is up.

Probably for the first time in your chase cycle this type of debtor feels threatened, and that is what convinces them to pay. But please remember, this threat has nothing to do with aggression, and everything to do with the mindset of the debtor. The 'won't pay' debtor does have a psychological payment trigger that will eventually induce payment, and this trigger is usually the involvement of a third party in the collection process. That is why collection agencies are successful, where your own in-house credit controllers are not. It has nothing to do with who is the better collector, and everything to do with the level of escalation. So swallow your pride and harness the power of this important collection sector.

Once our in-house collection cycle has been completed I always move to a collection agency, as my next level of contact. I accept that a letter from a collection agency, or a solicitor will have a similar affect on the debtor's psyche, but the collection agency will only charge me for the debt it collects, whereas a solicitor will charge me irrespective of whether the debt is collected or not. You should also remember that legal firms make their money from suing people, they do not make money from collecting debt at £1.50 a time. Before I alienate the entire legal profession let me clarify things and say that I am not anti-solicitors. I think they provide a valuable and necessary service within the debt collection arena, but not at this stage. A solicitor will not converse with your debtor, or resolve queries that emanate from their legal letter, not at £1.50 a time anyway – if they did they would go out of business. But collection agencies will fulfil this role, because the only way they get paid is by collecting the overdue debt. Let us now take a detailed look at how a collection agency should operate.

Collection Agencies

Many years ago collection agencies used to sell their services using a voucher system, which you paid for up front, then redeemed each time you passed an account to them for collection. Thankfully, this type of system has now virtually disappeared, and the golden rule today is: *never pay up front for collection services.* You should only pay a collection agency based on results. This way they remain focused on the job at hand, and are more eager to succeed.

Even though you are handing your accounts out to a collection agency, this does not mean that you lose control over the way they are chased. The collection agency is working for you, and you should agree a chase cycle with them and monitor their performance to ensure they follow it. Providing you offer standard thirty-day credit terms, your debt will already be at least sixty days old before you hand it out to a collection agency. The last thing you want is for them to take a further sixty days to complete their chase cycle. The collection agency that I use has agreed to chases our debt in the following way:

- An initial letter is sent within 24 hours of receipt of instructions.
- Forty-eight hours later a first call is made.
- Seven days later a second call is made.
- Seventy two hours later a final application is sent threatening imminent legal action.
- Seven days later the account is passed legal, providing I have authorised this action.

Within a three-week period we have moved from initiating third party collection action to instigating legal action. There are obviously occasions where this process may take longer – for example, where a debtor raises a payment query, or if the debtor has agreed to some form of instalment plan. But the point I'm making is that you should remain in control of the collection process. The agency may advise you on what they consider is the best course of action, but the decision remains yours. You will be held accountable for the collection of your company's debts, so it is important that you remain in control of the collection process at all times.

When choosing a collection agency it is always worthwhile taking up references from other companies who use them. Any reputable agency will be willing to give you a list of clients whom you can approach. You should also make sure that the Agency is licensed for debt collection under the Consumer Credit Act 1974, and also registered with the Office of Fair Trading.

Having chosen to use a collection agency, you now need to decide at what age to hand debt out to them. My advice would be to hand the debt out while it is still relatively collectable. After all that is what you want them to do. I hand debt out at around sixty-three days from invoice date. By this stage we will have completed our in-house collection cycle, so I don't see any point in delaying further. Continuity is very important when collecting debt. Having placed pressure on your debtor by stating you will hand their account out to a third party if payment is not received, you should maintain the pressure by doing exactly that.

After their final application, the collection agency should always seek authorisation before proceeding with legal action. This is important, because once you proceed with legal action your costs will rise rapidly, and you need to make sure it is cost effective to proceed in this way. If a debt is less than two hundred pounds in value, it may not be cost effective to proceed with legal action.

Choosing a collection agency that is right for you is a personal matter. However, I would recommend that you observe the following:

- Only use an agency that operates on a 'no collection, no fee' basis.

- Do not agree to any 'close-out' or 'file' charges. They are simply a back door way of obtaining money without collecting the debt.

- Constantly monitor the performance of your collection agency. Providing the debts are clean, free of queries, a seventy per cent strike rate should be achieved.

- Make sure you set the agency's collection time-frame to suit your needs.

- Make sure that the agency ask the debtors to pay you direct. If payments are made to the collection agency, make sure they are paid into a client account. This account will be protected if the agency goes into liquidation, and you would still receive your money in full.

- Use an agency that incorporates telephone calls within its chase cycle. Do not use an agency that simply runs a letter chase cycle. No matter what they say, they will not be successful.

- Make sure the agency is registered with the Office of Fair Trading, and licensed for debt collection under the Consumer Credit Act 1974.

The collection rates charged by collection agencies are, by their very nature, index-linked, and therefore do not need to be increased. As inflation causes the cost of your goods and services to rise, the value of the debts you send to the collection agency will also rise. This in turn leads to an increase in the value of commission the agency receives when it collects the debt. The following example for Cogg & Co shows this trend in action. For simplicity's sake in this example, and not reflecting actual rates, I have assumed that:

- Inflation in 2006 is running at 4%
- The sale price of 1,000 widgets in Jan 2006 is £10,000
- The sale price of 1,000 widgets in Jan 2007 is £10,000 + 4% inflation = £10,400

In January 2006 Cogg & Co sold 1,000 widgets to Won't Pay Engineering at a cost of £10,000. Having exhausted its in-house chase cycle they handed the debt out to Collections Are Us, who were successful at collecting the debt and charged a

4% collection commission. The cost of the collection was therefore £400 (£10,000 x 4%)

In January 2007 Cogg & Co sold a further 1,000 widgets to Won't Pay Engineering at a cost of £10,400 (£10,000 + 4% inflation). Once again the account was handed out to Collections Are Us, who collected the debt and charged their 4% commission. The cost of the collection this time was £416. (10,400 X 4%) The £16 increase in collection commission, year on year, is equivalent to a 4% rise in the cost of widgets due to inflation.

If a collection agency tries to raise the level of commission it charges, it can only be for one of the following reasons.

- The collection agency originally set their collection charges at an uneconomic level to obtain your business. Now having achieved that, they need to increase their charges to make your business profitable.

- They decide that it's worthwhile taking the risk of increasing their commission charge to enable then to increase their profits, while hoping they can justify this to their customers.

- The collection agency is not controlling its own costs properly, and tries to get its customers to pay for its own inefficiency.

- The company is trying to expand too quickly and does not have the necessary capital to finance this expansion.

- The collection agency is not performing very well and its poor collection results means it can't earn enough commission to cover its trading costs.

- The collection agency is loosing clients and failing to generate new business.

All of the above scenarios should cause you concern, and I would suggest you have a serious discussion with your collection agency if they try to increase their commission rates.

Measuring Performance

Having chosen your collection agency the next step is to monitor their performance. The first step is to decide how frequently you wish to carry out this monitoring. I would suggest you do this on a monthly basis. That way it's not too intrusive, but frequent enough for you to maintain control of the process. This monitoring process should take two forms:

1. You need to measure the number of accounts you are handing out to the agency, because this is an indication of how successful your in-house process is

2. You need to measure the collection performance of the agency itself. Remember, having your accounts grow old in their hands is just as costly as having them grow old in yours.

Measuring how much debt you send to the collection agency is an important measurement for the reason stated above; therefore it's surprising how many credit managers get this measurement wrong. In many cases you will find companies measuring nothing more than the monthly change in the level of debt that is with the collection agency. Unless your sales levels remain static, month after month, this type of measurement is useless. You need to measure collection agency debt in conjunction with your monthly sales levels. However, you don't send your debts to the collection agency as soon as they are generated, so you need to compare the agency debt against the relevant sales month. This measurement should be carried out on a percentage basis as follows:

Month	Sales	Debt With Collection Agency	Copllection Month	Percentage of Sales
Nov-06	£5,000,000	£250,000	Jan-07	5%
Dec-06	£5,750,000	£287,500	Feb-07	5%
Jan-07	£6,000,000	£300,000	Mar-07	5%
Feb-07	£6,250,000	£312,500	Apr-07	5%
Mar-07	£6,500,000	£325,000	May-07	5%
Apr-07	£7,000,000	£350,000	Jun-07	5%

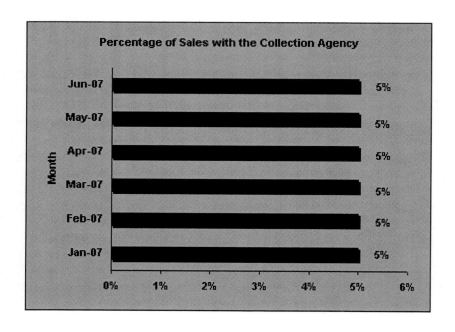

Fig 6:1 Collection agency debt for No Change Ltd

80

Month	Sales	Debt With Collection Agency	Collection Month	Percentage of Sales
Nov-06	£5,000,000	£250,000	Jan-07	5.0%
Dec-06	£5,750,000	£255,000	Feb-07	4.4%
Jan-07	£6,000,000	£265,000	Mar-07	4.4%
Feb-07	£6,250,000	£270,000	Apr-07	4.3%
Mar-07	£6,500,000	£275,000	May-07	4.2%
Apr-07	£7,000,000	£280,000	Jun-07	4.0%

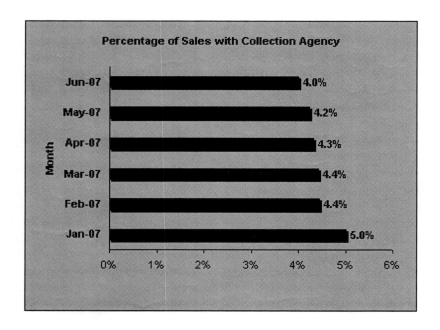

Fig 6:2 Collection agency debt for Getting Better Ltd

Month	Sales	Debt With Collection Agency	Collection Month	Percentage of Sales
Nov-06	£5,000,000	£250,000	Jan-07	5.0%
Dec-06	£4,750,000	£240,000	Feb-07	5.1%
Jan-07	£4,500,000	£235,000	Mar-07	5.2%
Feb-07	£4,250,000	£225,000	Apr-07	5.3%
Mar-07	£4,100,000	£220,000	May-07	5.4%
Apr-07	£3,700,000	£205,000	Jun-07	5.5%

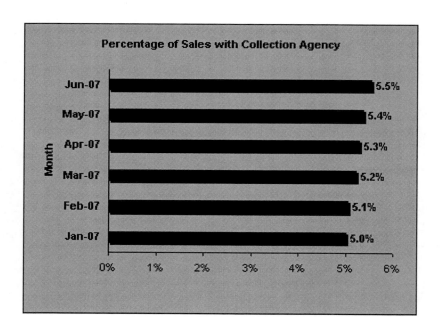

Fig 6:3 Collection agency debt for Getting Worse Ltd

The second element of measuring performance, relates to measuring the effectiveness of your collection agency. Once again this is not a straightforward process, and the golden rule is to measure the number of accounts that have been collected, and not the value of the debt collected. Unless all of your debtors owe you the same amount of money, which is highly unlikely, then large value debts could distort this measurement. Measuring the number of accounts collected will give you a pure success figure; however, you must remember to deduct any accounts with the collection agency that are in query before carrying out this measurement. The collection agency should not be penalised because you have not resolved outstanding queries with your debtors.

When reporting on your collection agency's success you should measure the number of debts collected, the number of debts sent legal, and the number of debts that have gone bad. Fig 6:4 shows how this report should be presented.

Collection Agency Performance Analysis	
Total accounts handed out in June	175
Less accounts closed out	10
Less accounts in query	5
Total Live Accounts	160
Accounts paid in full	120
Accounts placed legal	37
Accounts written off	3
Accounts still being chased	0
Total	160
Percentage of accounts paid	75%
Percentage of accounts placed legal	23%
Percentage of accounts written off	2%

Fig 6:4 Collection agency analysis

Having agreed on a format for these reports, the next decision you need to take is when to run them. If you invoiced all your customers on the same day each month this would be a simple process, because we would be handing them out to the agency on the same day. But as most of us invoice on a daily basis a little more thought is required. If you follow the chase system stated in the previous chapters, you will be handing accounts out to the agency on a continual, and possibly daily, basis. To get an accurate measurement of success we need to allow the agency enough time to complete their full chase cycle, therefore, I always report these figures at the end of the month following the month the debt is handed out. This means that I am reporting on collection debt, which is on average, 45 days old. This gives the agency plenty of time to complete their chase cycle, and gives more accurate results.

In-House Collection Agency

As stated earlier, collection agencies are successful because of the psychological thought process they trigger in your debtors mind. Therefore, it follows that an in-house collection agency should create this same psychological reaction.

If the in-house agency is going to be successful, you need to convince your debtors that a third party is contacting them. To achieve this illusion you need to make sure of the following:

- A separate letterhead is used for the collection agency.
- A separate phone number, fax number, and email address are used for the agency
- Separate staff are used for the agency's collection and customer-facing work.

A Separate Letterhead

The letterhead should look effective with a separate company logo. Do not set the letterhead up with a fictitious limited company as this is very easy to check up on. You should register your in-house agency as a separate limited company, but make sure it has a different registered office address and a different set of Directors.

Dedicated Telephone Lines

A couple of dedicated telephone lines need to be used. These lines should appear to be direct lines and not rooted through your company switchboard. A dedicated answer machine should also be used for these lines. On no occasion should these phones be answered by any of the credit control team, if the debtor recognises their voices the game will be up.

Dedicated Staff

The in-house agency obviously needs its own dedicated staff. These staff should try and divorce themselves from the main trading company. A collection agency will only have a limited knowledge about the working practices of their clients, so if their staff display a detailed knowledge this might arouse suspicion.

There is no doubt that an in-house collection agency can be as effective as an outside agency, and while it's appealing to retain total control of your collection process, there is one other element that needs to be considered. Running an in-house collection agency is expensive as can be seen in fig 6:5, and unless you hand enough debt out to a collection agency to make the process cost effective, then there is little point in following this path.

Outside Collection Agency	Worthwhile	Not Worthwhile
Number of Accounts per month	350	100
Average Value per month	£850	£500
Average cost of collection	3%	3%
Annual success rate	85%	85%
Value of debts handed out per annum	3,570,000	600,000
Revenue collected per annum	3,034,500	510,000
Cost of collection per annum	91,035	15,300
In-house Collection Agency		
Salary senior credit controller	25,000	25,000
Salary junior credit controller	21,000	21,000
Employment costs	23,000	23,000
Holiday cover	5,000	5,000
Telephone costs	2,750	1,250
Stationery	600	360
Postage	1,000	600
Costs incurred per annum	78,350	76,210
Comparison		
Outside agency cost	91,035	15,300
Less in-house agency costs	78,350	76,210
Gain/(Loss) using outside agency	12,685	-60,910

Fig 6:5 Comparison of in-house and external collection agency

Solicitors

Many collection agencies are associated with a firm of solicitors. However, while this makes the instigation of legal action a simple process, there is no guarantee that these solicitors will be the most cost effective option for your legal collection work. Once a collection agency has completed its chase cycle there is no reason why you should not close out your action, and find your own firm of debt collection solicitors. Don't place too much reliance on the collection agency's recommendation, as they probably receive some form of retainer from the solicitors they recommend. You should always ask the solicitors for independent references and a list of their charges, so that you can make an informed decision.

The firm of solicitors your company uses for its other corporate affairs will probably be the wrong choice for your debt collection needs. In the majority of cases debt collection work is not a complicated process; however, it is time consuming and that means expensive. If you pass debts out for legal action on a regular basis, you would be advised to choose a firm who specialise in debt collection work. These solicitors will almost certainly use a computerised litigation system which can be dealt with quite adequately by a legal executive, thereby reducing your legal costs. A fully-fledged solicitor would only be needed if the case reached a seriously defended stage. But cost is not the only issue; you need a firm that can offer a quick and effective service. One point of warning: it is costly to change your solicitors in the middle of a legal action, so take your time and make the right choice.

Using the courts for debt collection is a costly business, even more so since the Woolf reforms were introduced, which are discussed in greater detail in the next chapter. If you become involved in a seriously defended action your costs can escalate very quickly, so before you proceed make sure this is the only option open to you.

As with your collection agency, you should monitor your legal cases on a regular basis. You also need to monitor the individual cost of each case to make sure it is still cost effective to continue with the action. It is my personal belief that legal action should only be used as a last resort, and collection agencies should always be the first port of call. This is not because I believe they will be any more successful, but because I know they will be more cost-effective.

Some Useful Contacts

Collection Agencies

Commercial & Trade Credit Agencies
2nd Floor
Broadway House
Trinity Place
Bexley Heath
Kent
DA6 7BG
Tel: 020 8303 0194
Contact: David Hood

Inter-Credit International Ltd.
4th Floor
South Point House
321 Chase Road
Southgate
London
N14 6JT
Tel: 020 8482 4444
Contact: Brendan Glover

Debt Collection Solicitors

T G Baynes.
Broadway House
Trinity Place
Bexley Heath
Kent
DA6 7BG
Tel 020 8301 7653
Contact: Richard Seadon

7

Using The Courts For Debt Collection

Legal action is a serious business, not only for your debtor but also for you, so always remember this is not a step to be taken lightly. Before you enter this process make sure you have exhausted all other options, otherwise you will suffer the wrath of the Court. The English legal system does not like being used as a debt collector, particularly since 26th April 1999. It was on this date that the Woolf reforms brought about the first change to our Civil Justice System in 124 years. The two basic objectives of the reform are:

1. To limit the number of legal actions the Court has to deal with, by trying to encourage both parties to resolve their differences prior to taking legal action. To further encourage this action the reforms have prevented both parties from recovering costs in simple small claim actions, unless either of them is deemed to have been unreasonable in bringing their case.

2. To make sure that if legal action is taken both parties are operating on a level playing field.

The litigation process will be controlled by ensuring the Courts deal with the actions justly. This basically means:

- ensuring that both parties are on an equal footing

- dealing with the case in ways that are proportionate to:
  - the amount of money involved
  - the importance of the case
  - the complexity of the issue
  - to the financial positions of each party
  - ensuring that the case is dealt with quickly and fairly
  - ensuring that an appropriate share of the Court's resources are allotted to the case

Bearing these objectives in mind, let us now look in greater detail at the process of collecting debt through the English courts.

Prior To Issuing Proceedings

There are three rules that need to be followed before entering legal action.

1. The claimant needs to make sure they have done everything possible to recover their debt prior to proceeding with legal action. Any departures from a proper chase protocol will need to be explained to the court. If the judge feels that the reasons given for the departure are not sufficient, the courts could impose cost penalties against the claimant for premature issue.

2. Make sure you have a well-documented case before you proceed. You won't convince the courts that you have a just claim unless you have evidence to prove your debt.

3. Make sure you are prepared to see the case through to the end. It can be expensive to withdraw from a case half way through a legal action.

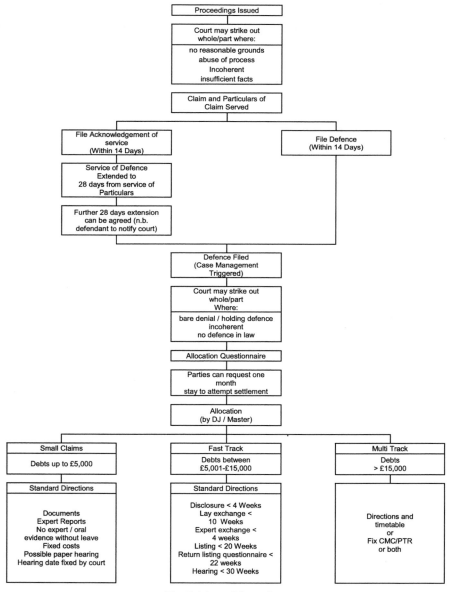

Fig 7:1 Legal flow chart

93

Starting Proceedings

At present, debt recovery actions below the threshold of £15,000 must be issued and heard in the County Courts, unless the disputed claim is of such a complicated nature that it needs to be heard by a High Court Judge. Debt collection matters are rarely that complicated, so there is a good chance most of your actions will be processed through the County Courts.

All actions, whether in the High or County Courts, will begin with the issuing of a standard claim form. When issuing a legal action the solicitor acting on your behalf will need to supply the defendant, (your debtor), with a detailed 'particulars of claim'. The particulars of claim can either be served on the defendant with the claim form, or separately within a 14-day period. This means that you need to supply to your solicitor full details of your claim, along with any supporting documents, prior to instigating the legal action. There is no point in starting legal proceedings without making sure you have the necessary documentation to back up your claim. Your particulars of claim should include:

- a complete statement of the nature of the claim
- a statement of the value of the claim
- a statement of truth.

It is important that the 'statement of case', formerly known as the pleadings, is written in plain English so that the defendant can fully understand the claim being made against him. Clarity is one of the prime requirements under the Woolf reforms.

It is also important to remember that a statement of case that is not coherent, or does not contain sufficient details to prove a legally recognisable claim, is likely to be struck out by the courts.

As stated earlier, one of the main purposes of the Woolf reforms, was to reduce the number of actions being processed by the courts, thereby freeing up court time and reducing the long delays that used to exist in bringing matters to the County Court. To achieve this goal the Woolf reforms empowered judges to take a greater role in the management of cases, and this process starts by making sure the claimant has a case and the defendant has a viable defence.

Another major change brought about by the Woolf reforms, was the introduction of the 'statement of truth'. The statement of truth is a declaration by the appropriate party that the information stated in their documentation is true to the best of their knowledge. The statement of truth is an important part of the new reforms as it allows the statement of case, and witness statements, to be used as evidence at hearings. These statements take on the same importance as giving evidence under oath, and therefore can reduce the need for witnesses to give long, time-consuming evidence in court. To ensure the validity of the statements of truth, any deliberate attempt to mislead the court will be treated in the same way as lying on the stand under oath: a committal hearing for perjury. The punishment for perjury is either a large fine or imprisonment, or in some cases both.

Entering a Defence

Once the claimant has issued his particulars of claim the defendant can react in one of three ways:

1. Pay the full debt and costs to the claimant or their solicitors.
2. Issue an acknowledgment of service
3. Enter a defence.

Issuing an acknowledgement of service will allow the defendant 28 days from the service of the claimant's particulars of claim, to enter a defence. Under the Woolf reforms, the defendant can no longer enter a spurious defence to try and delay matters, as he has a legal obligation to state:

- which allegations in the particular of claim are denied

- which allegations can not be denied or admitted and therefore require the claimant to prove
- and finally those allegations that the defendant does admit.

The Woolf reforms require the defendant to give reasons for his denial, or his statement of events. He can no longer waste the Court's time, and delay the point at which he actually has to pay, simply by stating he does not agree with the claim made against him. Lord Woolf did not believe that everyone was entitled to their day in court, especially if their sole purpose was simply to delay the inevitable. This was an important part of Lord Woolf's strategy to reduce the backlog of cases that existed prior to his reforms.

As with the claimant's particulars of claim, the defendant's defence also has to be detailed, coherent, and written in plain English.

Lord Woolf's thinking behind the changes in the presentation of a claim and defence was to encourage both parties to think very carefully about their dispute. Hopefully, this would lead to a greater number of disputes being resolved prior to litigation.

Disclosure of Information

As stated, one of the main threads running through the Woolf reforms is the need to reduce the amount of court time wasted on actions that could, and should, have been resolved a lot earlier. Lord Woolf tackled this problem by changing the rules of discovery, and thereby stopping solicitors, or defendants acting on their own behalf, from delaying matters by asking for irrelevant information during the discovery process.

The Court now has full discretion on the level of disclosure it deems necessary. The items that the Court is likely to require you to disclose are as follows:

- The documents on which your case relies

- Specific documents requested by the judge
- Any documents that adversely affect your case
- Any documents that support another party's case.

This list of disclosure must be accompanied by a detailed statement of truth that includes:

- details listing the extent of the search carried out to locate all relevant documents
- an acceptance that the party has understood the particulars of disclosure placed upon him
- certification that to the best of his knowledge he has carried out his duty to disclose.

Summary Judgment

Another change brought about by the Woolf reforms, is that a claimant can now apply for Summary Judgment in the County Court. The Courts also have the power to grant Summary Judgment against the claimant or defendant at their own discretion. The Court will take this action if they believe that the claimant has no real chance of proving his case, or the defendant has no real prospect of defending the action.

The Courts can also issue a stay on proceedings, for an initial one-month period, if both parties are willing to try to negotiate a settlement. The Court does not need the consent of the various parties to proceed along this line. Once again Lord Woolf's thinking was to encourage the different parties to talk to each other, rather than use the Courts to resolve their differences.

Allocation to a Track

If your debtor puts in a defence to your claim the Court will allocate the action to a specific track. In order for the Court to allocate the case to the correct track they will send each party involved a detailed questionnaire, which must be completed and returned within 14 days.

As part of the allocation process the Court will consider the following points:

- the contents of the statement of case and any need for clarification
- whether to strike out the action or defence, or whether to award summary judgement
- possible stays for negotiation
- a trial date.

When allocating the case to a specific track, the Courts will take into account the following factors:

- the value of the claim and any counterclaim
- the remedy sought
- the complexity of the case
- the number of parties and potential witnesses
- the amount of oral evidence that will need to be heard
- the probable length of the trial
- the views of the parties.

Each track has a value assigned to it and this will be the first consideration of the Court when allocating cases. However, it should be remembered that the calculation value is based on the disputed value of the claim, and not the total value of the claim. A case cannot be allocated to a track of lower value unless both parties agree. Whilst it is possible to ask the Court to allocate a case to a higher track than the value determines, any arguments lodged with the Court would have to be of considerable merit, and both parties would have to agree to the change.

The Small Claims Track

As its name suggests the small claims track is for claims of small value. Any normal debt recovery claim up to the value of £5,000 (excluding interest and costs) will be allocated to this track. The process for this track is similar to that of the old small claims procedure, in that only limited costs will be recoverable. Cases will be held in public, and there is no right of appeal, unless the affected party can show a mistake of law, or serious irregularities affecting the proceedings.

The Fast track

The fast track is applied to more serious cases, where the value of the claim falls between £5,001 and £15,000 and the trial can be disposed of in one day or less by the Courts. Once a case has been assigned to the fast track, it will take approximately 30 weeks for the Court to hear the case.

Multi-Track

The multi-track path will be allocated to cases where their value exceeds £15,000, or the value is between £5,001 and £15,000 and the trial will last more than one day. The case management may take place in the County Courts, or The Royal Courts of Justice, but trials are likely to take place at Civil Trial Centres. The Courts will closely manage trials in this band. There may also be the need for a greater number of case management conferences. As cases in this band are of a higher value, the parties will be able to claim a greater level of costs, however, the process of proportionality will still apply.

Enforcement of a Judgement

Many people believe that once they achieve judgement in their favour, the job is done. However, this is sometimes the easy bit; you still need to force the debtor to pay. There are a number of ways to enforce a judgement and the most common of these are now discussed in greater detail.

Warrant of Execution

A warrant of execution can be issued on judgements between £5 and £5,000 in the County Court. However if you wish to enforce the judgement in the High Court you can have the judgement transferred for a small fee. The only real benefit of transferring the action to the High Court is that the High Court Enforcement Officer, rather than the County Court Enforcement Officer, will carry out the enforcement. As the High Court Enforcement Officer tends to be a sheriff, and the Sheriff works on a commission basis, he may have a greater motivation to recover your money; whereas a County Court Bailiff is paid a flat wage and therefore may be less motivated. The thing to remember here is that neither the Bailiff nor Sheriff will be successful in recovering your debt if your debtor has no money or goods to levy on. There is no difference in the actual enforcement process whether it takes place in the High Court or County Court. Anything over £600 can be transferred up for enforcement, but it is usually recommended that only debt above £1,000 be transferred to the High Court for the purpose of enforcement.

The Enforcement Officer will visit the debtor's premises in an effort to obtain payment. If the debtor is unable to discharge payment, the Enforcement Officer will attempt to seize goods to cover the cost of your debt, removal and disposal. Providing the Enforcement Officer does not believe your debtor will abscond, he will probably take walking possession over the debtor's goods. This means the debtor will be given a period of time, usually seven days, to clear the debt before his goods are seized. Once walking possession is taken over the debtor's goods he is not allowed to dispose of them until the full debt has been discharged, or a third party claim has been accepted.

Having taken walking possession, it is not unusual for the Enforcement Officer to receive a third party claim on some or all of the goods seized. This means that a third party is claiming ownership of the goods. This third party could be a relative, a hire purchase or leasing company, or in the case of a limited company, the debtor himself, if he claims he personally owns the goods levied on and is only loaning them to the limited company. If this claim is verified the goods cannot be seized to clear the debt. If you wish to challenge a third party claim you will need to notify the High Court Enforcement Officer, who will issue an interpleader summons. However, this action can be costly and, unless you are sure you can overturn the third party claim, you should probably avoid this process.

The Writ of Fi-Fa

The writ of Fi-Fa is the High Court equivalent of the Warrant of Execution. As stated above the only difference between the two will be the value of your debt, which will be above £15,000, and the fact that the High Court Sheriff will carry out the enforcement.

Third Party Debt Order (Garnishee Order)

Third party debt orders are used when a debtor does not pay the judgement debt but you believe he has the funds, or is owed the funds, to enable him to do so. A third party debt order is usually issued against your debtor's bank, effectively forcing it to freeze any money in your debtor's account up to the amount of your judgement debt. Your debtor will then be informed of the situation, and given up to the hearing date to discharge your debt of his own accord. If he fails to do so his bank will be instructed to pay the money directly into Court.

It is not possible to garnishee an overdrawn bank account, so timing is of the utmost importance. If you know your debtor is expecting a large cheque in two weeks you should delay your action to coincide with its arrival.

The information needed to issue a third party debt order, such as the bank account number, account name, and branch sort code, can be obtained from any recent cheques you have received from your debtor, or any dishonoured cheques that have been returned to you. This information should also be recorded on your credit application form.

It is also possible to issue a third party debt order on another company or individual who you know owes your debtor money. This will force the creditor to pay the money owed to the Court and not to the debtor.

Attachment of Earnings

As its name suggests, this type of enforcement is useful against a debtor who is in regular employment. In these cases the attachment of earnings order is served on the debtor's employer. The order will instruct the employer to deduct a given amount from your debtor's salary each month, which is then paid into court. The order will last until your debt costs and interest have been recovered in full.

The drawback to this type of enforcement is that it only works on individuals who are employed by a third party. It is of no use against a debtor who is self-employed, or a limited company, and can be frustrated by the debtor changing employer.

Oral Examination

This sounds like something from the medieval debt collection guide, but unfortunately it's not. This isn't really a type of enforcement; it's a way of discovering what assets your debtor has. The court will instruct the debtor, if an individual, or the proprietor or director of your debtor company, to attend Court and give details relating to the financial health of their business.

The information gleaned from this type of examination enables you to clarify the options open to you for the recovery of your debt. As stated, the oral examination is unlikely to lead directly to the payment of your debt, unless your debtor has something serious he wishes to hide. The oral examination is useful to help decide whether it is financially viable to continue with your enforcement action.

Charging Order

The charging order is a long-term method of enforcement, unless you are really lucky and your debtor is trying to dispose of his property. A charging order will only be effective against a debtor who owns his own property, and if the property is jointly owned, usually only a restriction against dealings will be allowed.

You will often find that your charge is third in line behind:

1. the building society with which your debtor has his mortgage;
2. the debtor's bank to secure his overdraft or loan facilities.

As stated this is a long-term type of enforcement and you will not receive your money until your debtor sells his house, and only then if there is enough equity in the house to settle any prior charges once the mortgage has been cleared. A charging order can also be lodged against any shares owned by the debtor.

Liquidation & Bankruptcy

Although it is hard to consider the actual process of liquidation and bankruptcy as types of enforcement, the threat of this action certainly falls into this category. This is the ultimate action you can take to recover your debt, but not one that should be taken lightly. This type of action is not cheap and should only be used where you are owed a large sum of money, and against a business whose assets are greater in value than its liabilities.

The only way in which a bankruptcy petition can be issued is through:

- non-compliance with a statutory demand
- an unsatisfied writ of Fi-Fa or warrant of execution.

The threat of bankruptcy tends to be more successful than the threat of liquidation and this is because bankruptcy is aimed at the individual, which makes it more personal and therefore more effective. The Directors of a limited company are not affected personally by liquidation, unless it can be proved they have been trading illegally, whereas bankruptcy will affect the personal life of the debtor and his family.

8

Assessing The Risk

The days of bank and trade references have almost passed. With today's access to instant information there's a new champion on the block. Credit status reports, credit limits, and a detailed credit history of both Company and Director, can be yours within minutes, all brought to you through an on-line, credit checking system. And while these reports may allow even the uninitiated to make a credit decision, it still makes sense to understand how the business information companies analyse the data.

Ratio Analysis

Ratio analysis is used to measure a company's current performance against previous years. Analysis of the ratios listed below, and especially of any recent changes in the ratios, provides a good indication of a company's current trading performance. And it should be remembered that a company's ability to meet its future liabilities is directly linked to its historic trading performance.

To illustrate the ratios discussed in the following sections we consider the examples of two companies, On the Up Ltd and Going Down Ltd, whose financial trading history can be summarised as follows:

105

On The Up Ltd

	2003	2004	2005	2006	2007
Sales	500,000	600,000	700,000	800,000	900,000
Purchases	300,000	400,000	500,000	600,000	700,000
Current assets	440,000	520,000	600,000	680,000	760,000
Current liabilities	360,000	410,000	470,000	520,000	560,000
Working capital	80,000	110,000	130,000	160,000	200,000
Stock	200,000	210,000	215,000	220,000	225,000
Debtors	190,000	230,000	260,000	290,000	310,000
Creditors	320,000	365,000	420,000	460,000	480,000
Gross profit	45,000	57,000	70,000	84,000	99,000
Net profit before tax	20,000	27,000	35,000	44,000	54,000
Retained earnings	200,000	216,200	237,200	263,600	296,000

Going Down Ltd

	2003	2004	2005	2006	2007
Sales	500,000	600,000	700,000	800,000	900,000
Purchases	300,000	400,000	500,000	600,000	700,000
Current assets	390,000	440,000	500,000	550,000	590,000
Current liabilities	410,000	500,000	600,000	670,000	725,000
Working capital	-20,000	-60,000	-100,000	-120,000	-135,000
Stock	190,000	210,000	230,000	260,000	285,000
Debtors	130,000	170,000	200,000	230,000	270,000
Creditors	240,000	255,000	290,000	320,000	356,000
Gross profit	25,000	20,000	16,000	13,000	5,000
Net profit before tax	11,000	8,000	4,000	1,000	-4,000
Retained earnings	30,000	34,800	37,200	37,800	33,800

Fig 8:1 Financial statements for On The Up Ltd & Going Down Ltd

106

Current Ratio

The current ratio is measured by dividing a company's current assets such as (debtors, stock, cash) by its current liabilities such as (creditors, overdraft, short-term loan). This measurement shows a company's ability to repay the money it owes. A ratio in excess of 1.0 is good, and means that the company could immediately repay every penny it owes. Ratios below 1.0 suggest a company may be experiencing cash flow problems, although companies can trade quite happily with ratios as low as 0.8. However any company whose ratio falls below this level should be treated with great caution.

If we look at the trading statement for On The Up Ltd in fig 8:1, we see the company is trading with a current ratio of 1.36 (current assets £760,000/current liabilities £560,000). If this company is not paying your account on time it's because they are cash managing your money and not because they have cash flow problems.

On the other hand if we look at Going Down Ltd, we see the company is trading with a current ratio of 0.8 (current assets £590,000/current liabilities £725,000). Although the current ratio for this company is well below the desired level it is still above the level where you need to be seriously concerned.

It is worth noting that the current ratio measurement can be a little misleading, especially if the company is carrying a high level of stock, which cannot easily be turned into cash in the short term. Therefore, with this in mind, the 'acid test' ratio may be a little more revealing.

Acid Test Ratio

The acid test, also known as the quick ratio, deducts stock from the current assets. This can seriously alter the financial view of a company as can be seen with Going Down Ltd.

If we look at the latest acid test ratio for On the Up Ltd, we see that it equates to 0.96 (£760,000–£225,000/£560,000). Although there is a significant reduction this figure is still at the top end of your control band, and therefore should not cause you any worries.

107

Unfortunately, the figures for Going Down Ltd do not look so good. The acid test ratio for this company shows the ratio figure declining to 0.42. (£590,000–£285,000/£725,000). This would suggest that Going Down Ltd is suffering from a downturn in trading and is carrying a high level of stock as a result. This figure is a long way outside your control band and suggests the company must be suffering from severe cash flow problems. And as you will remember from the very first page of this book, insufficient cash flow is the reason most company's cease to trade.

When analysing a company's trading results, it should be remembered that financial results are nothing more than a snapshot of a company's finances at a given point in time. Although the figures look bad for Going Down Ltd, they could be misleading. Maybe the last reporting year was unusually bad. To get a true picture of what is happening to a company you need to measure its ratio analysis over a number of years. This will provide you with a trend that will show you if the company's position is improving or declining. The tables in Fig 8:2 show the profit trends for On The Up Ltd and Going Down Ltd. Which company do you think you should be dealing with?

Profitability Ratios

Although a company may be profitable this is no guarantee that it is going to continue to trade. Although profitability plays an important part in a company's survival, poor cash flow can still lead to its demise. However, if a company has been trading at a loss for a number of years it is unlikely that its directors or its bankers will continue to finance its trading. For this reason profitability ratios are a good indication of whether your money would be at risk if you offered credit facilities. The two ratios I use most often to measure profitability are:

- Gross profit margin = gross profit / sales (%)
- Net profit margin before tax = net profit before tax / sales (%)

Gross Profit Margin	2003	2004	2005	2006	2007
On The Up Ltd	9.0%	9.5%	10.0%	10.5%	11.0%
Going Down Ltd	5.0%	3.3%	2.3%	1.6%	0.5%
Net Profit Margin before tax	2003	2004	2005	2006	2007
On The Up Ltd	4.0%	4.5%	5.0%	5.5%	6.0%
Going Down Ltd	2.2%	1.3%	0.6%	0.1%	-0.4%

Fig 8:2 Profit margin analysis

The tables above show that On The Up Ltd has increased both its gross profit and profit margin consistently over the last five years. This is a strong indication that the company is being well run and that its costs are under control. These figures, taken in conjunction with the acid test ratio, suggest this is a very sound company.

The figures for Going Down Ltd do not look so good. Its profitability has fallen consecutively for the last five years. Although the company has made profits in the past, its present loss-making position, taken in conjunction with it poor acid test ratio, suggests this is not a company you should be trading with.

Two other ratios that may be of interest measure how quickly a company collects its debt and how quickly it pays its creditors. If these two ratios are out of sync with each other, and creditors are paid a lot more quickly than debts are collected, this could lead to cash flow problems:

- Days Sales Outstanding (DSO) = (debtors/sales) x 365
- Days Purchases Outstanding (also known as Creditors Ratio) = (creditors/purchases) x 365

9

Harnessing Modern Technology

Back in the mists of time, a debt collector's bag of tricks would have included:

- a large club, always good to administer rough justice

- the lash, a painful form of punishment administered with a whip, good for causing pain and humiliation, as the punishment was often performed in public to act as a deterrent

- the lead necklace, a punishment administered in debtors' prison, which would end in an agonising death through lead poisoning unless the debtor's family or friends cleared his debt.

Thankfully time has moved on to a less barbaric society and modern technology offers us a subtler, though probably not as effective, set of tools.

Email

The debt collection process starts with the issuing of an invoice, while, for the customer, his payment process starts with the receipt of an invoice. Therefore to enhance your collection process it makes sense to get your invoices to your customers as quickly as possible. The easiest and cheapest way to achieve this is to send your invoice by email. This process delivers three advantages for your company:

1. Your costs are reduced because you do not have to print the invoice, you do not have to fold it and put it in an envelope, and you do not have to pay postage to send it.

2. There is no delay in the debtor receiving your invoice. An invoice emailed Thursday night, will be received Thursday night, not in the post on Monday morning.

3. Your customer will not be able to delay payment by claiming he hasn't received it. If the email is not received, perhaps because your customer has changed his email address, it will bounce back to you and you can then take the necessary action to ensure delivery is completed. (I just love being proactive)

Many customers will not pay an account until they receive a statement that they can reconcile against their own accounts. If, as I do, you have a large number of statements to be sent out, this can prove to be a time consuming business. By emailing your statements your customer receives them as soon as your accounting period has closed, which should help to speed up payment from the majority of your customers. As with the emailing of invoices, your debtors cannot delay payment by claiming they have not received your statement. Emails are delivered to a specific person's desktop; they do not get lost in the post or mysteriously disappear from the fax machine. If you request 'read receipts' you can also see the actual time the email was read. It is also possible to add a voice message to the email, explaining standard items that appear on your statement, which may reduce the number of incoming queries you receive when statements are sent out.

One area where I am not so keen to use email is when issuing a debt recovery letter. I believe the visual impact of these letters grabs the debtor's attention and therefore adds to their perceived importance. It's hard to achieve the same level of impact in an email. Yes you can put marching ants around important phrases, or make the words 'Debt Recovery Enforcement Department', flash like a demented neon sign, but I think this makes the letter look tacky not serious. However, having said that, I believe the emailing of letters is useful if your debtor is based abroad, especially if they trade in a country where the post is notoriously unreliable. Emails are especially useful for chasing payment when your customer reside on the other side of the world. Time differences have historically made this type of collection difficult, but emails are breaking down these barriers and allowing an effective collection process.

Emails can also be used to provide hard evidence of your chase process. It can be very productive to confirm a telephonic conversation by email, especially if you felt the debtor was just paying lip service to your request for payment. Seeing an agreement in black and white psychologically makes it real, and that's the first step to getting your debtor to pay.

The World Wide Web

Over the years I have spent a lot of money on my company's behalf trying to track down a debtor's whereabouts, or make a connection between a company and a particular individual. This process is now a lot easier thanks to the immense amount of information that can be found on the Internet. Most businesses these days will operate a website as part of their sales process, and these sites are ideal places to pick up new trading addresses and contact phone numbers. They may also contain registered office information, which may not have been made available to you if your debtor is trading under a product name. These web sites may also include a list of customers your debtor trades with, which will be useful if you wish to obtain an independent reference on the company. I know these companies shouldn't give you information on your debtor without his agreement, but if he has listed them on his website as points of reference that is probably enough.

Working From Home

I have taken the advantages of modern technology one step further, to allow my entire credit control team, and part of my sales ledger team, to work from home. This is a truly innovative step that has produced benefits for both the employee and the employer. By eliminating the need to travel to work the employee benefits from eliminating travelling and subsistence costs. On average for my staff this equates to a saving of £2,000 per annum per person. One of my credit controllers has even been able to move hundreds of miles away while still retaining the job she loves. As an employer we have benefited from a reduced office space requirement, reduced employee costs, a more motivated team, a drastic reduction in sick days, and last but not least, a *ninety five per cent increase in productivity*. I could go on for hours about the benefits of this process, but that's a whole different book.

10

Outsourcing

Outsourcing is a process where you hand the responsibility for the collection of part or all of your debtors' ledger out to a third party organisation. These companies will contact your debtors, usually stating that they are your company, in an effort to recover debt. In some cases they will also carry out your sales ledger process as well, as the two functions are closely related.

So why would a company outsource its debt collection process? Personally, I wouldn't. Providing you operate a professional credit control process in-house, the only possible benefit I can imagine is a slight reduction in the overall costs associated with your collection process. However, these reductions are by no means guaranteed, and there are risks attached. I fail to see why any medium to large-sized company would wish to hand control of its most important asset out to a third party.

Before committing to an outsource agreement make sure you examine the contract closely. Some of the things you need to look out for are listed below:

- the length of the cancellation period
- the cost of the service
- any hidden costs such as file charges, admin charges, close-out fees.
- the process of transferring cases to a collection agency footing, and the associated costs for this service
- make sure all money is paid directly to you and not banked by the outsource company. There is no point

in them collection your money more quickly and then delaying forwarding it on to you.

As stated, these are my personal views. However, I am prepared to admit that there are occasions where outsourcing may be of benefit, and these are discussed below.

Outsourcing for Small Businesses

A small business that only employs a few members of staff, and has a fairly small customer base, would probably benefit from outsourcing its credit control process. It is unlikely that such businesses would require a full time credit controller. This means that the credit control process is usually either given to a general accounts person, or performed by the owner of the business who has better things to do with his time, or not carried out at all. Whichever scenario applies, one thing is for certain: the credit control function will not be carried out in a professional way. In these circumstances outsourcing companies can be of value. They should offer a professional service with their costs tailored to your needs. If your collection requirement is only three days a week that is all you should be charged for. Through economies of scale outsourcing companies should be able to provide a cost-effective yet productive service. Because the small business in the scenario above does not have an effective credit control function, the outsourcing company should be able to improve on the speed of their collections and therefore provide it with much needed working capital.

Outsourcing for Special Projects

If a large company, such as a publishing company sells one of its magazines, or decides to close it down, the customers related to this product tend to feel there is less urgency to clear their debt. In this type of situation there is a benefit associated with hitting these debtors hard with a concerted collection effort. Unfortunately, this concerted effort is not always something that can be built in to a company's normal collection process, so an outsource process to cover this type of situation is often the most cost effective answer.

The same principle can also apply to cover for maternity leave, where the employee concerned may have worked part time, or reduced hours. This type of role would be difficult to fill with temporary, or long-term contract staff, as these types of employees usually want to work five days a week. Outsourcing companies can fill this void quite happily through their economies of scale and only charge you for the hours you need to cover.

Outsourcing companies can also help if you need to generate a large amount of cash flow over a short period of time. However, if you are running a successful in-house collection process, the benefits here are likely to be very small, as you should already be collecting all available debt. It should be remembered that slow debt collection that is due to problems with internal sales processes would not be improved by handing debt out to an outsourcing company.

Fines and Fees

Outsourcing also works well where there is a lot of small value debt and/or where customer retention is of no importance. The type of debt that could fall into this category are motoring fines, court fines, or unpaid congestion charges.